Live with more purpose

# Listen To Your Heart

## She Knows Best

Miriam H. Ezell

ISBN: 1480149748
ISBN-13: 9781480149748

Library of Congress Control Number: 2012919998
CreateSpace Independent Publishing Platform
North Charleston, South Carolina

This book is dedicated to
the woman seeking ….
seeking for more time, more energy,
more peace

# Table of Contents

# Introduction

**"I believe that everyone has at least one book in them. In fact, each of us are walking 'stories' just by being alive. I have a book in me and I have a story to tell. I have a story that needs to be told, otherwise I would not be here."**

**— Laurie Beth Jones, author of THE PATH**

I, too, have a story that needs to be told. My story is alive in me and I live it out every day.

My story is a journey of discovering my authentic self, purpose, and passion. It began, as most journeys do with heartbreak and disappointment. I had a life-long dream of being a wife and a mother. Ever since I can remember I played with dolls. I have pictures of me, at a very young age, sitting at the little table in my playroom with my doll and tea set.

As a child, I had watched my mother make our house a home: wallpapering, refinishing furniture, having family dinners of 20 or more, sewing, and planning birthday parties. She loved being a wife and a mother and it showed.

Watching the movie "Cinderella" only made me hungry to meet "Prince Charming" and live happily ever after.

After meeting my "Prince Charming" and being married for 17 years, THAT is when I realized my dream would NOT come true. I would never be a mother.

When Tim and I were not getting pregnant, tests were performed. I remember the afternoon Tim called me at work and said he talked with the doctor and the results were back. We would not be able to have children. What?!!! The news hit me hard. I felt like a knife was sticking in my chest. I couldn't breathe.

We would never come up with a name for a child. We would never see what our child would look like, nor what type of personality the child would have. We would not be going to his or her graduation or planning a wedding. We would not be "blessed" with a child.

I handled the news by getting busy. I went back to school and worked on a second degree. Then I spent years studying for the CPA (Certified Public Accountant) exam. After that, I started studying for the certified financial planner exam.

I hated holidays like Christmas. I wanted to crawl into a hole from December 1 to January 3. Christmas is for kids and we didn't have any. We did not put up a tree. Mother's Day and Father's Day were extremely difficult and Tim and I declared those as "Mimi" Day and "Timmy" Day and celebrated by doing something we wanted to do and honored each other in that special way.

During this time (around our fourth year of marriage), we started working with our church high school youth program. We were involved, we went on retreats and mission trips. Being with the teenagers seemed to fill the void. We met some fabulous kids along the way and still remain in touch with some of them as they have grown up and now have children of their own. We worked with this youth program for 10 years.

Years went by pretty fast, and at age 40 I realized the doctors were right. I wasn't going to be a mother. We were finished working with teens and I was forced to take a strong, hard look at myself and ask, "Now what?"

As a result of asking myself that question, my journey of "now what?" began. I had to discover that if I was not going to be a mom, then I had to ask and find out who was I going to be.

My journey to discover the unique, authentic person that I am has lead to this story, this book. I share my story because this journey of discovery is not just available to me, but available to every woman. That means YOU!

Each of us is unique; each of us is creative. We all have an authenticity about us that needs to be shared with others, with this world. We, as women, add value. It is NEVER too late to be a blessing or to leave a legacy.

**"Everyone's story deserves to be told, whether it is with pen and paper, fiction or fact, paint on canvas, or with the pulse of a sewing machine. We move from solitary to connected as we weave our truthful tales out into the world."**

— **Vivienne McMaster, photographer**

I choose pen and paper as I write, "Listen to Your Heart: She Knows Best" to weave my truthful tales into the world.

My journey led to finding my uniqueness and what I did with it has made me into a more fulfilled woman, a more contented woman, and a woman who wants to be a part of her community giving back and encouraging other women to live life on purpose and NOT by default.

What does it mean to live by default? Here are some questions to ask yourself that fall into the "living by default" category:

- Do you spend time with friends who drain you, just because it seems like it would be too much trouble to make new friends?

- Do you work at a job you can't stand but stay with it because you need the cash flow?

- Do you walk into your home and look at all the clutter; it is overwhelming to pick it up, so you let it be?

- Do you constantly put other's needs first before your own?

- Do you refuse to take time out to recharge your battery and to have fun?

- Do you lack passion and purpose in living?

- Do you feel drained, tired, and are you gaining weight?

We, as women, fall into what I call, "survival" mode. We take care of family. We allow others to fill our plates. We settle. We feel guilty when we don't do what others think we should. We take on tasks that don't fit our abilities and gifting and wonder why we are criticized for our work. We try to do it all. We take care of everyone else and put ourselves on the back burner, then we crash and burn. We lack confidence and listen to gossip, which only leads to hurtful feelings. Because of our frustration, we get sick, we gain weight, we get depressed, we no longer take care of our physical being. We no longer feel that we add value and we are not heard. The list goes on and we spiral down into a feeling of hopelessness.

Please don't misunderstand me. I am not encouraging you to be selfish. I do not want you to think this book is all about ME, it is not. It is about setting boundaries, taking time out and taking care of yourself, which is necessary. It is about making good, healthy choices. It is about asking yourself questions that speak to your heart and soul and answering them honestly. It is about making decisions that result in a better person. It is about finding your authenticity; what makes you sing, what makes you laugh, what speaks to your heart and soul. These things will bring you energy and will encourage you to continue to be the true nurturer, caregiver, cash flow earner that you were called and are called to be.

**"Don't ask yourself what the world needs; ask yourself what makes you come alive. And then go and do that. Because what the world needs is people who have come alive."**

**— Harold Whitman**

My wish is that after you read this book, you step back and with determination, say to yourself, "I am tired of living by default. I will choose to live on purpose; and will do something about it today."

You may be living in an abusive home and need to leave. This is a tough decision and a huge step to take. You may be working at a job that is draining you and giving you headaches because you do not want to be there. Leaving this job takes courage and is a big step to take. You may be overweight and as a result have health issues. Choosing a different lifestyle of eating and exercising is a major decision and a tough step to take. You may be in debt and overwhelmed with bills. Taking charge of your cash flow is a necessary decision.

Or, maybe you had a dream, like me, and that dream did not become a reality; and now you are lost and unfulfilled. Or maybe that dream is still alive in you and you don't know how to take steps toward fulfilling your dream.

By reading this book you are taking the first step to changing your life, turning your life around, and making the effort to start fresh and new.

It is NOT only my desire for you that you find a life of purpose, but more importantly, that you know it is *God's* desire for you! You can come alive! You can and will experience it! The choice is yours and the choice needs to start now.

# The Book that Spoke to My Heart and Soul

Have you ever read a book you couldn't put down? That is what was happening to me. I was waking up at 5 a.m. in the morning to read the next "thought" for the day. I was getting out of bed to have quiet time. I couldn't wait to read the words that were jumping off the page and speaking to the depths of my heart and soul.

The book, "Simple Abundance: A Daybook of Comfort and Joy," by Sarah Ban Breathnach, was a bestseller in 1995. In September 1996, it arrived in my home from a dear friend, Morri, as a birthday gift. At the time, I thought, "how nice," thanked her for the gift, and placed the book on the bookshelf. At 34 years old, I placed the book on the bookshelf because I didn't think I needed this book. Inside the book Morri wrote, "Dear Mimi, Happy Birthday to you! Here is wishing you a life of SIMPLE ABUNDANCE."

So, how did I come to love this book so much that it was getting me out of bed in the morning? Why am I making such a big deal over this book? Because this book transformed my life and became my foundation for who I am and who I am supposed to be. It changed my thinking; it changed my behavior.

This transformation took place over many years; it did not happen overnight. This has been a process in the making. Let me share with you this journey, this discovery, and how it came about.

## My life was actually a MESS!

I was a mess! I was getting ready to turn 40, entering the next decade of my life. I was a CPA with my own CPA practice. I was a wife, a daughter, and a sister. My husband and I had just resigned from 10 years of working with the church youth group because we thought we were "too old" and the teens could not relate to us anymore.

At 40 years of age, the realization hit me hard like a ton of bricks. I had known for years I would never get pregnant, but it finally dawned on me: I would never be a mother. I guess the doctors were right all along. I started asking myself, "If I am not going to be a mother then what am I supposed to do with my life?" I was looking for purpose. My volunteer role had ended and we were no longer working with the teens, I lost my ministry as well.

My role as a CPA was just that – a role – it was  not fulfilling enough for me. I did not like who I saw in the mirror. I had no essence. I had no joy. Something was missing, but I did not know what or how to find that missing piece. I was even telling friends, "When I turn 50, I want to do something totally different, totally unique." I was giving myself permission to find this uniqueness at the age of 50 - but why wait till I am 50? Fifty was 10 years down the road.

I had no purpose, no goal, and Satan was attacking pretty hard with negative thoughts in my head. It was the voice of self-sabotage that was consuming me and draining me of energy.

While growing up in the church and being a part of a Christian family, I had always heard that God had a plan for me based on the verse in Jeremiah 29:11 that says, *"For I know the plans I have for you declares the Lord, plans to make you prosper and not for evil. Plans to give you a future and a hope."*

"Really?" I asked myself. I had no idea what those plans were at 40 years old. At 40 I was halfway through my life and I still didn't know the plans God had for me. I knew there was something missing in my life, but I couldn't put my finger on it.  I didn't know how to find this "missing piece" or what this "missing piece" even was. I knew there had to be more to life than what I was experiencing.  What I was going through felt like a black cloud hanging over my head.

I wanted Jesus to come sit at my kitchen table over a cup of coffee and just tell me, "Miriam, these are the plans I have for you ….." Then, I would know.  Then, I could move forward on my "personal life plan" and all would be well. But, it doesn't work like that. I am left alone to figure this out. Now that I look back on it, I am glad I had to figure this out on my own. I started my discovery journey and it turned out to be a fabulous journey.  Sure it had its ups and downs, but it was an adventure just the same. My mother often says, "Every day is an adventure." How true that is.  On this discovery journey, before I could do what I needed to do, I needed to know who I was.

## Vision board

At the beginning of this journey, during a visit to see my mom, she introduced me to the same book, "Simple Abundance."  She was reading it because this book was given to her as a gift.  During my visit, she began sharing with me what she was learning from the book, and she had finished a vision posterboard (aka vision board) that was recommended as an exercise in the book. A vision board is a posterboard usually made up of photos, clipped magazine images and words that symbolize one's personal vision or goals. Mom was having a great time putting it together and seemed so enthusiastic about the project!  Mom was in her 60s and was discovering things about herself she did not know.

When I saw her completed vision board, I was excited and wanted to do one of my own. What impressed me about this vision board, was that mom was recognizing what she loved and what she wanted.  This was a new concept to me. I realized I didn't know what I loved or wanted.  Being married for several years, the conversation in my head was, "If I identified what I wanted, would my husband even allow me to have what I wanted?"

After visiting mom for the weekend, I came home and took the book off the shelf and wanted to see what the excitement was all about. The book had been collecting dust for four years.

As I turned the page to the Forward of the book, this is what I read:

> *"Often people attempt to live their lives backwards: they try to have more things, or more money, in order to do more of what they want so that they will be happier. The way it actually works is the reverse. You must first be who you really are, then, do what you need to do, in order to have what you want."*
>
> – Margaret Young

Wow! "You *first* must be who you really are." That piqued my interest. I realized, I didn't have a clue as to who I was, but I *did* know that there was definitely a desire in my belly to find it. Often, as women, we don't know who we are because we spend our energy elsewhere like family and careers. Or, like me, I was listening to my family, who were telling me, "You should do this, you should do that…."

I was also taught as a child that our purpose, as children of God, is to glorify God. Ok, I get that. But, that sounds so vague. Could you be a little bit more specific? At this point in my life, I was just existing — going from work to home, home to work, taking care of the household chores and errands. Big whoopie doo! That was not exciting me, nor was the fact that I was walking around with a black cloud hanging over my head. I don't think that was glorifying God either.

In John 10:10 Jesus says, *"For I have come that you might live life, and have it with abundance."* Jesus says abundance, not a humdrum life of boredom, not a life of just so-so. I wanted a life of abundance because this sounded so peaceful, so refreshing, so relaxing. What exactly does abundance mean? It could mean many different things to different people, but what did it mean to me?

Ban Breathnach, the author of *Simple Abundance*, wanted to write a book that would show her how to reconcile her deepest spiritual, authentic, and creative longings. She knew she was not the only woman herding through real life as if it were an out-of-body experience. (AMEN to that!)

Anne Morrow Lindbergh, an American aviator and author, recognized the demands on us as women. She was the wife of the famous pilot, Charles Lindbergh. She had five children and one month out of her summer she would become a recluse at the beach with the sole purpose of recharging her battery. Lindbergh describes it this way in her book "Gift from the Sea":

> "For life today in America is based on the premise of ever-widening circles of contact and communication. It not only involves family demands, but community demands, national demands, international demands on the good citizen through social and cultural pressures, through newspapers, magazines, radio programs, political drives, charitable appeals and so on. My mind reels with it. What a curious act we, women, perform everyday of our lives. It puts the trapeze artist to shame. Look at us. We run a tight rope daily, balancing a pile of books on our head. Baby carriages, parasol, kitchen chair, still under control. Steady now! This is not the life of simplicity, but the life of multiplicity that the wise man warned us of. It leads not to unification but to fragmentation. It does not bring grace; it destroys the soul. This is not only true of my life, I am forced to conclude; it is the life of millions of women in America."

Ban Breathnach knew she wasn't the only woman frazzled, depressed, or worn out. She wanted so much – money, success, recognition, genuine creative expression – but had absolutely no clue as to what she truly needed. She was a woman in desperate need of "Simple Abundance."

I felt this way too! I was in desperate need of simple abundance, but didn't have a clue how to get it or what that looked like or felt like. Ban Breathnach wrote about "reconciling your genuine creative expression" – love that too! I did not think of myself as creative, so IF there was a creative expression in me of some kind, I wanted to find it. As Lindbergh pointed out in her book, "I have a choice of how I want to live my life."

# The CHOICE

I have a choice? I can determine how I want to live my life? This was a new concept after living day to day going through the motions and allowing my life to be dictated by whatever demands fell on my plate. I was determined to go on a discovery journey. What woman doesn't want simple abundance?! I want to connect with my authentic self, but how would I do that?

Then I started thinking, "What does it really mean to be authentic?" I know we are all created with uniqueness; we all have our own talents and abilities. But what does it *really* mean to be authentic and to find your authenticity?

When I first started reading the book, I struggled with the concept of giving myself permission to work on me. I was raised in a Christian family where the mindset is: you sacrifice, you serve — less of yourself, more of God. I had a grandmother who spent her time serving the Lord and doing for others, but I also noticed she did not know how to have fun. It appeared to me that she was always angry. She did not know the "joy of her salvation." She was out of balance. I wanted to work on me and also wanted balance with the Christian perspective of serving.

I was also taught that I needed to let my light shine. In "The Artist's Way," Julia Cameron tells us to turn on the "spiritual electricity." To me, to let my light shine means to allow Jesus to radiate through me. If I am a woman who is not content, who is angry, who is frustrated, who is trying to fit a square peg in a round hole, my light does not shine. If anything, I appear unapproachable and it turns people off, it turns people away. I want to shine. I want to learn how to turn on my "spiritual electricity."

## Journaling

Here I was waking up at 5 a.m. to read this book. The book, "Simple Abundance" is designed and organized as a walk through the year – 365 days – beginning on New Years' day. Each day has a thought, or reflection or a question to ponder. Each day builds upon the next. The purpose of the book is to reconcile your deepest spiritual, authentic, and creative longings. Reading the book and taking action was a journey, just like reading this one will be for you. Remember, it does not all fall into place at once.

Each day, it seemed like whatever the designated passage was for the day was exactly what I needed to read virtually verbatim. I felt like the book was written just for me. The words gave me a new perspective, a new way of thinking. The words were fresh ideas and gave me something to think about. Though there were many insights noted throughout the book, I am going to share with you a few of the ones that had the most impact on me.

My first step was to build a foundation. At the suggestion of Ban Breathnach's book, I started my journey with buying my first journal and began journaling. On the very first page, I wrote in big bold letters "The Year of Discovery." Just the effort of buying the journal and getting started excited my soul and opened up hope.

I had never journaled before and had never realized that you could learn so much about yourself through journaling. This was so powerful to me, that I have written a whole chapter in this book on the subject of journaling called, "The Power of Journaling."

## Find your creativity

Building on the foundation of the book and starting to journal, I was ready to excavate and "awaken the sleeping beauty within" as Ban Breathnach described. To excavate, she suggests you go on a "creative excursion." A creative excursion is something you do by yourself to listen and to see what speaks to your heart and soul and each excursion requires little or no money. Your biggest "cost" is time. This excursion allows you to discover a creative outlet that fits your personality— to awaken the dormant talents within.

My first creative excursion led me down the path of looking at magazines. I picked up a "Victoria" magazine and that was the beginning of the awakening of the "sleeping beauty" within. The pages were full of beautiful photos of fabric, buttons, and furniture all in soft whites and beiges.

As a result of reading the magazine and looking at the pictures, I fell in love with antique buttons. I was particularly attracted to the white, off-white pearl kind and started to repurpose picture frames by hot gluing buttons around the edges. I choose the pearl kind because they were shiny and added "bling" to a plain, boring object. Then, I found inexpensive handheld mirrors and started hot gluing buttons on the back. I was lost in my new found art project. I loved to seek jars of buttons at flea markets and antique malls. When a jar of buttons was found, I would come home and spend hours sorting them, looking at them, rubbing the smooth finish. I was hooked!

When sharing with a friend my enthusiasm about creative excursions, she suggested I put a booklet together. So I did! I have included this booklet in the chapter called "Creative Connection – You Are an Artist." I want other women to go on creative excursions to discover what resonates with them. I think this is a great exercise to finding that life of purpose – discovering what you love.

# What do you love?

Speaking of knowing what you love, in "Simple Abundance," I read about excavating one's self. What a concept! Excavating was hard because I had to "dig out" of the mindset that it is OK to work on me. After reading Sarah's insight of "knowing what you love," I asked myself – what do I love? What makes me sing? If I could do anything, what would that be?

These are exactly the questions I started asking myself at the beginning of my journey and here they are in this book, "Simple Abundance!"

By the way, these are also called "laser" questions in the life coaching profession. The question is designed to speak to your heart, soul, and gut. You seek the answers for *you*. No one else can fill in the blanks. You know what works best for you. When I started asking myself these laser questions, it was like opening the flood gates. As I wrote in my journal, it felt like a huge burden was lifted off of my shoulders. I started to breath. I started to relax. I started to smile. Here's what I came up with:

I love:

> Walks on the beach
> Drinking hot tea and visiting with a friend
> Coming home at the end of a day and getting a hug from my husband
> Reading a good book
> Working on an art project

These are just a few of the things that make my heart sing. When I made my list, I realized I was not spending enough time doing what I love, so I started to focus more on doing what I truly love to do.

What is it that *you* truly love? This is *not* a selfish question, but a *necessary* one. Finding the answers begin to open and awaken your spirit to find your true "authenticity." Give yourself permission to take a few minutes and write down your answer.

# What is it that I truly love?

_____

_____

_____

_____

_____

_____

_____

_____

_____

_____

## Style reflects the inner YOU

I think all of us, as women, deal with some dissatisfaction of how we look. When I open a women's magazine, the advertisements I see are about losing weight and face creams. They are all about looks, looking younger, being thin.

Remember, we as women are wonderful, talented, and smart. We add value to our families and community no matter what our shape, size, or color. This is really a hard concept to accept. I know; I have been there. I am just now finding a hairstyle that is authentic to me and not comparing my hair to every celebrity I see on the TV screen. I know I cannot have their hair; mine is thin. It is not long, wavy, and thick. It is not blond. I also have to remind myself that the celebrity has a hairstylist to style their hair for every event. Sometimes these stylists add hair extensions to give them that long, wavy, and thick hair. It is important to find out what hairstyle fits *you* for you, and not because a magazine or celebrity has decided it is a trend you should follow. The same is true of your style of dress.

Go shopping and try on lots of outfits. Find your style for your shape. If you struggle with this, there is a good book written by Stacy London and Clinton Kelly called, "Dress Your Best." London and Kelly are the hosts of the TV show, "What Not to Wear." I think you will find this book helpful. I am a pear shape; my upper body is smaller than my lower body. This means I have to wear blouses with color, shape, and design that draws the eye to the upper body rather than the lower. I learned this by reading the book.

Let me also encourage you to find your color. If you don't know what colors look best on you, visit a clothing store and hold colors up to your face. Does the color make you look pale or does the color brighten your complexion? There was a book written several years ago called "Color Me Beautiful" by Carole Jackson. This book helps you pick your season of color that looks best on you. The colors are divided up into the four seasons of the year.

Find what style works best for you. This will help you put your best foot forward, you will feel your best. It will boost your spirits and self-confidence. Be that wonderful person that you are created to be.

## Be in the moment

We tend to hear the word "balance." We are told we need to find "balance." Let me change that and say that whatever we are doing, wherever we are, just be present and in the moment. Just be! Just be 100% to that moment.

If you are with your children or grandchildren, be with them and give it your all. If you are with your spouse on a date, just give him your 100% attention. Be in the moment.

There is beauty all around me. I tend to be the type of person with so many tasks and goals that I don't stop to enjoy the moment. I am always thinking about the next thing, the next goal. Chop, chop; let's go! When this realization hit me, I started to slow down. I began to change my pace. I became happier and portrayed gratitude and thankfulness. I even step outside at the beginning of the day and just stop and soak in the moment. I breathe. I smell the air. I listen to the sounds around me. I am in that moment.

I was a runner for many years. I had to run every day. I had to get in those miles so I could write them down in my log book. Bedtime was early so I could get up early. I had to get home from work early enough to put in a few more miles. I remember once we had received a tornado warning and I still went out for a run. My husband thought I was insane. This is an example of being focused, but I was taking it to the extreme. At that time in my life, I was not in the moment.

Taking care of myself is very important to me and should be for you. Now I try to work out three times a week. I am no longer training for marathons, but still think it is important to take care of myself physically by working out with weights and walking. Even walking on the treadmill I am in the moment, feeling my muscles, and listening to my breathing. I am exercising with intention. I eat healthy. I drink plenty of water. I do all of that because being sick is an inconvenience to my schedule. Being sick keeps me from doing the things I want to do. More importantly, if I don't take care of me, I cannot help others. I would not have the strength or energy to give.

In the Spring we think of new beginnings, spring cleaning, putting our house in order. Living a life of purpose and abundance is about simplifying, bringing order, and bringing organization to your home and life.

On the May 6 page Ban Breathnach tells a story of two hideous lamps that sat in her house for more than 15 years just because they belonged to her grandmother. She hated the lamps and finally listened to her "authenticity" that said, "Well if you hate them so much, just get rid of them." So she did.

Reading Sarah's story of her grandmother's lamps makes me laugh and reminds me of a similar story.

My mother-in-law was fabulous at yard sales. She could find the most incredible stuff at the cheapest price. One day, she brought home this particular lamp she loved and thought it was great. The base was made of plastic and had a white, pearl finish, and the feet of the lamp were tarnished. My husband (her son) wanted the lamp so she let him have it. He brought it home and placed it on the mantle. For several days I looked at that thing and rolled my eyes. I thought this was the ugliest lamp I had ever seen. One day, when he was not home, I took the lamp out to his workshop, placed it on his workbench with a "yellow sticky" note on the lamp. The sticky note read, "I want to be with you in your workshop. I like it better out here." The next day the lamp appeared back in the house in the same place, on the mantle with another "yellow sticky" note. This note read, "I lied." I had to laugh. I took the lamp back out to the workshop and my husband got the message. I think we ended up giving the lamp away. Rather than fusing and fuming about this ugly lamp, I used my humor. I was beginning to use my authenticity.

## Ask for what you want

> "Ask and it shall be given to you; seek and ye shall find; knock, and it shall be opened unto you."
> -Matthew 7:7

Make your requests known. How does my husband know what I want if I don't make my requests known?

In 2006 I decided to attend the fast track program for coaching. One of the things I learned while attending training is to comprise a list of the things I wanted to a list of 10 items. So when I came home, I posted my list of 10 items I wanted on the refrigerator. My list consisted of things like: I want to spend more time at the beach. I want to work part time. I want to spend more time in my art studio and less time working in the yard, etc. It was late in the afternoon on the day I posted my list and I was working in the study on the computer. I heard my husband come in the door and walk around in the kitchen. Then, I didn't hear any footsteps, so I knew he was reading "the list." Suddenly, I heard him laughing, so I went to the kitchen to find out what was so funny; and he said, "No yard work?" "That's right," I replied. No more yard work for me; that is your job."

After that conversation, I was free to work on my art projects, which consisted of quilting and painting at the time. After several years of giving myself permission and having "permission" from my husband to work on my projects, I started to relax and feel freedom.

Something interesting happened though. After spending time working on my projects, I actually started working in the yard again because I wanted to! I actually wanted to be with my husband and help him. It was no longer a "have to." I started designing shrub beds and walkways. My husband loved what I was doing. With both of us working in the yard, we were able to get things done faster, and I still had Saturday afternoons to work on whatever I wanted.

During the writing of this book, which is six years later, I asked him what he actually thought of "the list." He said that he appreciated it because he is not a mind reader and the list let him know what I wanted. How simple is that?

So, I encourage you to post on the refrigerator your list. Maybe other members of your family will be inspired to write and share their list with the household. You will learn about them as you read their interests and what they want.

Still not convinced it's that easy to ask for what you want? Let me give you another real-life example. As I mentioned earlier, I was a frequent viewer of "What Not To Wear." What I loved about this TV series is that London

14

and Kelly would take an average person that did not know how to dress and teach them how to dress according to their body type and shape. The makeover would also include a new hairstyle and make-up session. I would come home every Friday night in time to watch this show. The transformation of each woman was incredible. When the woman came out at the end of the show with her new outfit, haircut and make up, my eyes would tear up, not just because she looked so incredible, but because she had an "inner shine." London and Kelly had brought out the "authentic" person. It was absolutely remarkable and the woman was so grateful for the transformation. This inspired me.

I announced to my husband that when I turned 50, I wanted to go to New York City and get a new hairstyle. I thought he would give me grief for just the thought, but he said nothing and was very quiet.

It was one month later when I turned 47 and my husband took me out for breakfast on my birthday. He asked me if I would like my birthday present. Dah! Of course! He handed me a white, business, size 10 envelope. I thought to myself, "Cash! Money to spend as I wish. I can go shopping! This is great." I opened the envelope and it wasn't cash, it was one sheet of paper.

I unfolded the sheet of paper and found a black and white print out of Nick Arrajo's website. Nick was the hairstylist in New York City giving these women their new hairstyles on the "What Not to Wear" TV Show. Written across the black and white website copy were big, bold, red letters that read: "**Appt. October 14 at 9:00 a.m.**"

"What? You made an appointment for me to get a new hairstyle in New York City? It is not even my 50th birthday." – (This is just one example of my husband's thoughtfulness.)

Plans were made to fly to New York with my dear friend, Morri, to accompany us. We spent the weekend in New York City and my "request" was granted – a new hairstyle, which by the way, was not that much different than my current style. My hairstylist in Huntsville, Alabama is pretty darn good and a whole lot cheaper.

My husband tells me, "all of your requests are granted." My response is, "that is because all of my requests are reasonable." I will have to admit that this was probably the most outlandish "request" I had ever made. All of my other requests do fall in the "reasonableness" category and I don't make that many.

## Do What Comes Naturally

I want each woman first of all to realize they are "chosen" and have been given an opportunity to use their creativity to prosper. Maybe that idea sounds too far out right now, but the thought is to use that creativity, that talent to make money and give back to the community or give back to the church. As the expression goes, if we do what we love, the money will eventually follow.

If we are forcing ourselves to do a job, a task that does not fit our personality, our style, our skill set, we become frustrated. We gain weight. We have headaches. We come home and kick the dog. We are in a word: miserable.

While working as an accountant at a CPA firm, I was assigned to perform an audit of a company's records. I hated this job. I hated the checklists and all the detail. This job was draining. I couldn't wait for 5 p.m. so I could head home. It wasn't long after I had taken on the job when the owner of the CPA firm called me into his office and said, "The jury is still deliberating and we don't think you will be with us next year." That was all I needed to hear. I went home and told my husband. The next day I showed up for work and said, "The jury doesn't need to decide; I quit." Every life experience, whether good or bad brings us to a necessary evaluation. That job was not a good fit for me. The work did not flow, it did not come from me naturally.

You, as a woman, add value. Your skill set is needed in this world. You have been designed with a specific skill set that is required. Do not bury that talent; do not ignore that skill set by saying, "I am not good enough," or by thinking of excuses.

## Thinking Back

As I reflected on my life, I began to wonder, why do we, as women, have to wait until we are 40, 50, 60 years old before we find out who we truly are? Wouldn't it be great if teenagers, especially girls, were given direction and focus to find their true self? Then they would be better prepared for their college life; they would be more in tune with what to study. They would be more self-confident and not "follow the crowd." They would be better prepared for their marriage. They would know what they were bringing to the altar on their wedding day, if they knew more about their authenticity.

When I was a teen, I did not have a mentor or anyone to help me make decisions or help me figure out what I should select as a major in college. Come to think of it, I didn't have anyone even to encourage me to go to college. There was an unspoken expectation for me to go to college. That this was a natural thing to do next after high school, but college or attending college was never discussed. The more I thought about it, the more I longed to do something about this.

I decided to write a class on finding your true, authentic self for teenage girls. I had just finished working with teens for 10 years. I knew their struggles. I knew that they needed to find their authentic selves.

The course had 14 lessons based on bible scripture. I used bible scripture because it is truth, and the principals work. Writing this class began to give me new purpose, new meaning, it was putting me back on track. Preparing this class was a needed objective and was speaking to my "authenticity." I called this class "I Got to Be Me." This course was designed to teach young ladies that they were created by God for God, and take them on a journey to discover more about themselves.

The lessons consisted of:

1. Intro – How this course came about
2. Who am I?
3. What are my talents and abilities?
4. Am I making good choices?
5. What does abundance mean to me?
6. What is inner beauty?
7. Am I thankful?
8. Am I content with whom God has created?
9. How do I develop a relationship with God?
10. Am I living in the Present moment – finding the path of JOY?
11. What is the importance of simplicity?
12. How do I manage my personal cash flow?
13. Who does God say that I AM?
14. After high school, then what?

Most of the lessons had homework assignments. I gave each young lady in class a journal with a blank cover. Their homework assignment for that week was to decorate the journal and bring it back the next week to class. It was interesting to see how each journal came to life with color, fabric, ribbons, buttons, stickers, etc. Each young lady was proud to display their "work of art."

After the course was over, I decided to have the girls fill out short surveys for feedback since this was my first time teaching on this topic. One of the comments I received was, "I loved how we related bible verses to every-thing in the class, even if we weren't learning about a specific scripture."

These are the responses to the question: What did you like most about this course?

"The friendliness in the class, and the warmth of love that floats around."
"Taking the personality test."
"Learning about journaling and I will continue to use a journal."
"Learning about myself."
"I really enjoyed making the Mr. Right page and learning about finances."

"I enjoyed everything about the class."
"Having permission to talk about yourself and getting to know yourself."

Writing and teaching this class put me back in my element and I was finding my true "authenticity." I was also learning that mentoring, teaching, and coaching these young ladies really spoke to me. I was learning to let my inner light shine. Preparing and teaching this class took me out from underneath the *dark cloud* that had been hovering over my head.

## Creative Longing

Remember at the beginning of my journey I wanted to find my "creative longing"? I did! My mother started taking watercolor lessons and I asked her to give me a demonstration because it looked fascinating. I commented to her that I would like to try it. So that year, she gave me watercolor paints and brushes for Christmas and then I found a friend who would give private painting lessons. The first couple of years were a struggle because my paintings were horrible. My first house looked like a cow. But I enjoyed the movement of the paint in water and kept at it. After four years of taking lessons and practice, my paintings had improved so much that I was now able to start selling them. More about this in the chapter "Creative Connection – You are an Artist."

## Continuing the Discovery

While in my early 40s and working as a Vice President of Finance, I began to wonder if this was it, was this where I was supposed to be? I could not stave off the yearning in my belly that said, "There has to be more." I was still on my journey searching.

Thanksgiving of 2005 I went to visit my mother in Massachusetts. She had just watched a show on Oprah that featured an author who wrote a book on life coaching. My mother went to the library and checked out this book for me to read during Thanksgiving break. I devoured the book. I did not realize that you could actually get paid for encouraging people and getting people focused on their goals. This really spoke to me on a deep level.

After my visit, I came home and started researching life coaching. I found Coach U out of Colorado and they were giving a "fast track" class in May 2006 in Atlanta. I signed up for the class and that is when my business, **Life by Design** was born. Although I attended the fast track class and started my life coaching company, it would take another two years when I was laid off from work that I started focusing on **Life by Design.**

## Summary

Once I figured out more about me and started treating myself with kindness, I was able to help others. I was able to take time for others and do it with a better attitude. When I started painting and selling my water color paintings, it made me feel appreciated. People really liked my work and bought it!

Life is a journey, why not live it with passion and purpose? That is what my business, Life by Design, is all about, working with women to find their authenticity, their gifts and using that to prosper and glorify their Creator – to live with passion and purpose.

I heard a minister define glorifying God as finding your gifting, what you are supposed to do, and then going out to *do it.*" That is it. Amen! Do what you have been designed to do. Live on purpose and with passion. I wonder what the world would be like if people were living on purpose? Would there be less drug and alcohol addiction? Would there be less domestic and child abuse? Would people actually look forward to going to work? Happy employees make for greater job satisfaction, higher efficiency, and more production on the job. Would work be called play rather than work? Would people make more income because they were doing what they were designed to do, excelling at it, and being rewarded for it? Would people be grateful and stop whining? Would people have better overall health and less obesity?

During my journey, I decided to attend a retreat in North Carolina called "The Path." The purpose of the workshop was to design a mission statement for life and for work. There were six women attending the workshop. I knew only one of these ladies because she came with me. Our first breakout session we were paired off with one other person and were instructed to share with that other person 10 significant things (called stepping stones) that had shaped us.

In my ignorance, I thought everyone attending this retreat had a spiritual or Christian background. I started sharing with this young lady, who I was teamed with, how God had played such a big part in my life. After I shared, she looked at me with tears in her eyes and said, "I want what you have. I want your faith." Now I was crying and I hugged her. I said, "You can; it is available to everyone." During the weekend retreat, she asked more questions and I gave her answers. I am hoping that after that weekend she was able to find the peace and faith she was looking for. She saw something authentic in me –my faith, my peace, and she wanted the same. What do people see in you?

Won't you join me in this discovery journey and find YOUR authenticity?

# The Power of Journaling

One day, I was standing at the kitchen sink washing dishes and I asked the Lord, "What do you want me to teach women through this book?"

Right away, Matthew 11 came to mind: "Come to me all who labor and are heavy laden, and I will give you rest. Take my yoke upon you, and learn from me; for I am gentle and lowly in heart, and you will find rest for your souls. For my yoke is easy, and my burden is light." – (Revised Standard Version)

I looked up the same verses in "The Living Bible," and this is what it said: "Come to me and I will give you rest – all of you who work hard beneath a heavy yoke. Wear my yoke – for it fits perfectly – and let me teach you, for I am gentle and humble, and you shall find rest for your souls; for I give you only light burdens."

Who wants rest? Wouldn't it be great if you could escape for one week? Go to a place to relax with no obligations, you don't have to cook a meal or do laundry, attend a meeting, teach bible class. Just go away and *rest*. Wouldn't that be a gift? Of course, it would take three of those days just to wind down and give yourself permission to rest and not worry about anything or anybody.

"The Power of Journaling" is about rest. When I started journaling, I discovered, it is my connection with my Creator. It is a two-way conversation with my Heavenly Father – Maker of heaven and earth. I put my yoke (my burdens) upon Him. The burdens that are hanging on my shoulders, the burdens that weigh me down like a ton of bricks, the burdens that keep me from living a life of purpose.

I recently spoke to a women's group about journaling and it was called –
What is your Goliath?

I began by reading the story of David and Goliath which is found in I
Samuel 17.

> "Now Saul, and all the men of Israel, were in the valley of Elah, fighting
> with the Philistines.  And David rose early in the morning, and left the
> sheep with a keeper, and took the provisions, and went, as Jesse (his
> father) had commanded him; and he came to the encampment as the
> host was going forth to the battle line, shouting the war cry.  And Israel
> and the Philistines drew up for battle, army against army.
>
> And David left the things in charge of the keeper of the baggage, and
> ran to the ranks, and went and greeted his brothers.  As he talked with
> them, behold the champion, the Philistine of Gath, Goliath by name
> came up out of the ranks of the Philistines, and spoke the same words
> as before.
>
> Goliath stood and shouted to the ranks of Israel, 'Why have you come
> to draw up for battle?  Am I not a Philistine and are you not servants of
> Saul?  Choose a man for yourselves, and let him come down to me.  If
> he is able to fight with me and kill me, then we will be your servants;
> but if I prevail against him and kill him, then you shall be our servants
> and serve us.'
>
> And David heard him.  All the men of Israel, when they saw the man,
> fled from him and were much afraid.  And the men of Israel said,
> 'Have you seen this man who has come up?  Surely he has come up
> to defy Israel.'  And David said to the men who stood by him, 'What
> shall be done for the man who kills this Philistine, and takes away
> the reproach from Israel?  For who is this uncircumcised Philistine,
> that he should defy the armies of the living God?  And the people
> answered him in the same way, 'So shall it be done to the man who
> kills him.'

When the words which David spoke were heard, they repeated them before Saul; and Saul sent for David. And David said to Saul, 'Let no man's heart fall because of him; your servant (David) will go and fight with this Philistine (Goliath).'

And Saul said to David, 'You are not able to go against this Philistine to fight with him; for you are but a **youth** (David, being a teenager, too young to be a soldier) and he (Goliath) has been a man of war from his youth.'

But David said to Saul, 'Your servant used to keep sheep for his father; and when there came a lion, or a bear, and took a lamb from the flock, I went after him and smote him and delivered the lamb out of his mouth; and if he arose against me, I caught him by his beard, and smote him and killed him. Your servant has killed both lions and bears; and this uncircumcised Philistine shall be like one of them, seeing he has defied the armies of the living God.'

And David said, 'The Lord who has delivered me from the paw of the lion and from the paw of the bear, he will deliver me from the hand of this Philistine. And Saul said to David, 'Go, and the Lord be with you!'

Then David took his staff in his hand and chose five smooth stones from the brook, and put them into his sheperd's bag; his sling was in his hand and he drew near to the Philistine.

And the Philistine came on and drew near to David, with his shield bearer in front of him. And when the Philistine looked and saw David, he disdained him; for he was but a youth, ruddy and comely in appearance. And the Philistine said to David, 'Am I a dog that you would come after me with sticks?'

And the Philistine cursed David by his gods. The Philistine said to David, 'Come to me and I will give your flesh to the birds of the air and to the beasts of the field.'

*Then David said to the Philistine, 'You come at me with a sword and with a spear and with a javelin; but I come to you **in the name of the Lord of hosts, the God of the armies of Israel**, whom you have defied. This day the Lord will deliver you into my hand, and I will strike you down, and cut off your head; and I will give the dead bodies of the host of the Philistines this day to the birds of the air and to the wild beasts of the earth; that all the earth may know that there is a God in Israel, and that all this assembly may know that the Lord saves not with sword and spear; **for the battle belongs to the Lord** and he will give you into my hand.'*

*When the Philistine arose and came and drew near to meet David, David ran quickly toward the battle line to meet the Philistine. And David put his hand in his bag and took out a stone, and slung it, and struck the Philistine on his forehead, and he fell on his face to the ground.*

*So David prevailed over the Philistine with a sling and with a stone, and struck the Philistine, and killed him; there was no sword in the hand of David. Then David ran and stood over the Philistine, and took the Philistine's sword and drew it out of its sheath, and cut his head with it. And David took the head of the Philistine and brought it back to Jerusalem."* – (Revised Standard Version)

What amazes me so much about this story is that one person made a huge difference, and this one person was just a teenager! Thinking back on this story, I ask you, "What is your Goliath? What shadows over your head like a giant? What is your biggest fear? What keeps you up at night? What is your biggest worry?"

The year 2008 was a hard year financially. It was my "big Goliath." On February 28, 2008, I was laid off from work and was now collecting unemployment. My husband and I had three mortgages to pay at the time. I journaled like crazy asking God to sell one of our pieces of real estate. I asked Him for cash flow to pay the bills. During that time I was journaling, I was totally at peace. I knew God would take care of things in his own timing. I just had to wait and see. I was turning this "battle" over to Him.

March 5, 2008 (six days after being laid off from work) this is what I wrote in my journal:

*Father – Good Morning. I will not let fear rise up against me. I will not let doubt rise up against me. I will not let debt rise up against me. Father, you know our situation; you know our cash flow needs. I want to be able to get out of debt and I want to be able to give back to YOU! I believe you are working in my life. I believe I will do what I need to do today – I will attack today. Father, you are my rock. AMEN.*

*June 10, 2008*

*Father, I am struggling this morning with the weight on my shoulders of debt. Please take this away. Please sell a property for me. Then I wrote, "Have faith in God when your prayers are unanswered. He sees and knows all the ways you have trod. Never alone are the least of his children. Have faith in God. Have faith in God."*

*Lord I know this is a test of faith. I hope I pass the test.*

**ANSWER TO PRAYER:** Thank goodness we had an emergency fund set aside and were able to pay the bills. In May of 2009 one of our properties sold in the worst housing market. *God* is good!

Going back to the Goliath story, in my opinion, David didn't just show up with a slingshot. The slingshot was the tool that God used to show His power and His glory. David showed up with confidence, with courage, with faith, with the remembrance that God was with him before when he fought off a bear and lion. So this giant was no big deal.

Today, we have a tool that we can use to fight our battles. Our tool is our journal. Journaling has become *my* tool to access God as my power source. Let me expound more on this.

# Why journal?

As I mentioned, when I journal, I begin with "Father …" Why do I journal? I journal because I am spending quiet time with the living God, my Heavenly Father, the Creator of heaven and earth. That is huge! I am spending time with the Almighty and guess what? He wants to spend time with me, with you. He loves us so much! Journaling to Him develops my relationship with him. He desires to have a relationship with you, too! This is not just available to me, but to EVERYONE who wishes to spend time with the Creator.

Why do I choose to spend time with my Creator? Because He created me. It is that simple. He knows what is best for me. Think of it this way. If you and I were designing a car, and this car was the fastest, slickest, and best on the market, people would be lining up on the street to buy this car. With this car, we prepared a "How to Manual" on how to take care of it, what oil to use, what tires you should put on the car, when to rotate the tires, what gas to use. All of these things are listed in the Manual so that the car will run at its maximum performance and will require less maintenance if the person takes care of it. That is what the Bible is, our manual for living. It has everything we need. The Bible is our "How to Manual."

Another reason why I journal is my Creator has a plan for me. I cannot see that plan, so I look to Him for guidance and wisdom to walk the path He has set before me. In Jeremiah 29:11 it states, "For I know the plans I have for you, declares the Lord, plans to make you prosper and NOT for evil, plans to give you a future and a hope. That when you call upon me, I will hear you, and when you seek me, you will find me when you seek me with all of your heart." I love that verse. Who doesn't want their Creator to listen to them and tell them He has plans to help them prosper.

Journaling helps you call upon *Him*. Journaling is seeking Him. You are seeking *His* wisdom, *His* guidance.

Someone will say, "But I don't have time to journal." I know we are all busy. In fact, many of us are *too* busy. Our time is limited. Time is precious. What we value is where we are going to spend our time and our *money*. If you value journaling and spending time with your Creator, you will find the time. Once you start, it will become an addiction and you won't be able to stop. Start small for five minutes a day and see where it takes you.

## How to Journal

First, you must purchase a journal. My journals range in the form of a nice hardback cover, a spiral bound notebook, or something artsy with a beautiful picture on the front purchased at a bookstore. I recommend the journals be lined paper. Personally, I cannot write in a straight line on a blank sheet of paper. I need lined paper.

Sometimes I will purchase a gold gel pen. This makes the letters sparkle on the page. It gives the page bling, bling which we, as women, like.

Create a "sacred space", a quiet place in your home with your favorite, comfortable chair. Your quiet place must have good lighting. It must be totally quiet – the dishwasher should not be running, TV is not on, no music, totally quiet. Your sacred space is where you meet your Creator every time. It becomes your meeting place.

You do not have to write in your journal for the purpose of being grammatically correct. It can have words crossed out or misspellings. Do not be a perfectionist about it. Just write.

You can even draw pictures if you wish instead of words. One of my friends journals with pictures rather than words. She is visually creative. This works for her. This is called art journaling and there is actually a magazine called "Art Journaling" for inspiration found in local bookstores.

I, personally, am a morning person. So I journal in the morning before anyone else is awake. I make coffee and sip on coffee as I write. I choose to write in the morning because I know I need God's guidance during the day. It is my way of saying I cannot live my life alone, without Him. I need Him.

Then I will read scripture from the Bible. Just a few verses and think, ponder over those verses. I open my journal and start with the date. Then the writing begins with, "Father – ". I start writing my conversation with my Heavenly Father and I write whatever is on my mind for that day. I call this "data dumping." I write about my frustrations, my fears, my goals, and my gratitude. I must put gratitude in my writing because I am thankful. I acknowledge that I am blessed and I don't want to appear as a whiner, always complaining, griping, and asking. I recently read that the first step to joy is gratitude.

I may write about the verses I just read. Can I apply them to my situation, to my life at this time? If so, then I will write what I just learned from the scripture.

I thank God even for the "uglies"; the things that are painful, hurtful, sorrowful.

So, whatever is in my head that morning, I write it down on paper, in my journal.

If you need a "kick start" to start journaling, you can purchase a devotional book or guided journal that will give you questions or inspirational text to read first and then write about what you read.

Write down what you learned by reading the devotional text or the thought. Write down what impressed you about the reading. Did you have an "aha" moment?

Sometimes what I read in the scriptures will answer a question I was previously thinking of! I will have a thought, a decision to make, a frustration, and then when I read my devotional for that day, it deals with that exact situation. It is amazing! And *yes*, I will have an "aha" moment.

Begin by journaling for five minutes. You will discover that once you begin and witness the results, five minutes is not going to be enough. Five minutes turns into 30 minutes and then before you know it, an hour has passed and you wish you did not have to get ready for the day. You just want to sit there and keep going.

Here is another idea that I do almost every time I journal. When I sit down to write, I ask this question, "Father, what do you want to teach me today?" Then I put my pen to the paper and just write. To give you an example, one of the lady's at church, who knows I love journaling, asked me to teach a class on journaling to young moms. I told her I would pray about it, which means, to me, journal about it, and this is how it went:

*June 21, 2011 – Why journaling? Father, what do you want me to tell these young moms about why they should journal? (This is what came to me as I put pen to paper), "My precious daughter, journaling is spending time with me. I long to be with my children. I love my children so much. Cast all your cares upon me for my yoke is easy. Bring me your struggles, your fears, your burdens and I will give you peace. For my word says; ask and it shall be given, seek and ye shall find, it also says in the book of Jeremiah that if you seek me, you will find me, that if you pray to me, I will hear you, for I have come that you might have life and have it with abundance – not so/so. I have created you with a uniqueness. I have created you to live a full, rich life. Don't listen to the voice of DEATH that wants to steal your joy. Satan is a liar and a thief. But listen to my voice; I am the good shepherd; my sheep know my voice. I speak LIFE. I speak energy. I empower my children, my daughters. I am light, in me there is no darkness. So share that with my children, my daughters, the moms. Moms need to hear my voice, they need my enthusiasm and energy. I know they are weary. I know their days can be long. They are raising precious ones."*

Wow! OK, amen to that! Thank you, Lord.

# BENEFITS of Journaling

Once you begin to journal, the following will begin to happen:

**You start making better choices.** Because you are taking the time to reflect and think through your choices before you act, you will find that your choices will be wiser because they come from an inner assurance. You may want to journal and ask yourself, "What are the pros and cons of this decision?" "How will this choice that I am about to make affect my life or the people around me?" Wisdom is the choice that the decision you make today will have a positive effect on tomorrow.

**Decisions will be based on strength and NOT on fear.** Fear is often a motivator, but it should not be when making decisions. We should not base our decisions on what other people think or how other people will react to our decisions. We need to make decisions based on what will work best for us. If we are *afraid* to do something, it is probably because we have never done it before and it is unknown. We have a fear of failure, embarrassment, or rejection. I look at those decisions as growing experiences and as challenges. OK, so what if I flop? I will learn from that decision and will try this same thing again and NOT make the same mistake twice. Listen to yourself and trust what you hear. Often times an authentic answer will come while you are journaling and your body will tell you whether it is right or not. By that I mean, your body will give you a sign; such as a stomach ache, an intuition, a gut reaction.

**Self-criticism will cease and you will begin to speak *life*.** I call "speaking life" positive reinforcement talk. An example of "speaking life" is telling yourself, "I am smart. I *can* do this. I will be successful." As opposed to "speaking death," which is negative talk. "Speaking death" might sound something like, "I am so stupid. I can't believe I just did that. I will *never* get out of debt. I will *never* be successful." "Speaking death" drains your energy, and slowly kills your spirit. Practice writing the positive words down in your journal. This will help to reinforce your words and thoughts.

**Gain confidence and self-worth.** As I journal my frustrations, fears, disappointments and "dump" it onto paper, I release it to my Creator. I can actually feel the burden come off of my shoulders and I literally feel like I am sitting straighter and taller in my chair. The burdens melt away and I feel more confident. My shoulders are held back and not drooping forward. As God reveals himself to you through your journaling, He will tell you He loves you and you are his cherished possession. You will begin to see yourself as your Creator does.

**You will be able to think clearly.** Because you are "data dumping," which means that what is in your head is being removed and placed on paper, you are de-cluttering your mind. Sometimes there is a lot rolling around in my head. Writing it down detangles the thoughts.

**You become grounded.** Becoming grounded means you stand up for what you think is right. You stand firm. You are not easily persuaded by someone else's comments or opinions. You know what is right for you. Again, you listen to yourself and trust what you hear. This new grounded confidence is gained through journaling.

**Your journals become written legacies.** As I am writing in my journal and I write about concerns, frustrations, and problems, it may be six months when I go back in the journal and look to see what I wrote and how that issue or problem was resolved. If it was resolved, I write in the margin how and when it was answered and I write it down in a different color pen so that it stands out on the page. I hope that when I am long gone, my nieces and nephews (since I don't have children) will take my journals and read them. They will discover more about who I was and what struggles I was dealing with. The journal also talks about experiences that I have gone through and what transpired. The journal will become a written legacy for my family.

**Journaling is a form of self-care and your battery will be re-charged.** We as women tend to fill up our plates and take care of everyone except ourselves. Taking time out for ourselves is not selfish, *but* necessary.

We need time out to re-energize our battery. This is what journaling does. It is time alone to think, to ponder, to be still, to be quiet, to dream. By doing this, our battery is recharged. We are ready to face the world again. Journaling will teach us how to rest in the moment.

Journaling strengthens your relationship with your Heavenly Father because it is communicating your thoughts, your cares, your frustrations, and your gratitude. Through journaling, you bring *all* of your problems to Him. This is a great way to spend time with God.

If journaling does all these things, it sounds like a "wonder drug" doesn't it? Who doesn't need or want these benefits? Sign me up!

## My Experiences of Journaling

One of my favorite journaling experiences was on March 10, 2008:

> Father – I keep thinking about this seminar (Calling All Women to Prosper). I keep waking up thinking about the words I would say. I want YOU so much to be in this seminar. I want so much for YOU to send the people that need to hear the message. You know my love language is words of affirmation, I need to hear from you that this is just what you want me to do.
>
> If I watch TV, I get scared and lose confidence. Father, I want to give back financially to your kingdom. I want to get out of debt. This is the fastest way I know. If I could give 30 seminars with 50 people, that would be awesome. I am so fired up! I am so encouraged! I am so blessed! So many people encourage me."

That is what I wrote to my Heavenly Father on March 10, 2008 – looking for words of affirmation as I plan on speaking and giving seminars. In February 2008 I was laid off from work, so my business, Life by Design, came into fruition, and now I needed to make income. I was REALLY looking for affirmation and looking for confidence.

That day, March 10, 2008 I received this note in the mail:

Dear Mimi (my nick name) -

What a wonderful lesson! From your expertise in money to your wonderful smile, which shows the light of the Lord and the love of the Lord in your life, the lesson was well taught and modeled. Because you and Tim show such love for others and such faith, you even brought folks to class. That is quite a testimonial to your lives. You also demonstrate to us all that you are willing to study and teach. That is such an example of what we learn through Elisha - God will help us greater than we can imagine if we just trust in Him and not ourselves. Thanks for being Mimi – a friend who loves the Lord.

Love, Margaret

On March 10, 2008 I asked for affirmation and words of encouragement in my journaling that morning. I received that note in the mail on the day I asked for it. *But* here is the amazing part about that note. The class Margaret mentions in her letter, where we were learning about Elisha, I had taught one year earlier. That note was one year old and I received it on the day I asked for it.

I called Margaret and asked her why I was receiving a note in the mail after it was written over a year ago. She laughed and said, "I found it in my purse on Saturday. I didn't know if I should mail it or not, but I did." I received that note on Monday, March 10, 2008, the day I needed it the most. Amazing! God can use anything and anyone to inspire and encourage us in a powerful way. This was one small way that He answered my request and proved He loved me. God is good. It amazes me how He works behind the scenes answering our requests.

So, on March 11, 2008, the day after I received the note, this is what I wrote in my journal in reference to that experience:

*Father – Wow! Ask and ye shall receive! You are so amazing! You are so good to me. Go ye therefore and speak. I will! Thank you, Lord for those words of affirmation.*

*Then I wrote the words to a song that popped into my head;*

*The secret of life is letting go. The secret of love is letting it show. In all that I do, in all that I say – right in this moment. The power of prayer is in a humble cry; the power of change is in giving my life and laying it down, down at your feet – right here in this moment. Take my heart, take my soul; I surrender everything to your control and all that is within me, I lift up to you and say I am yours and yours alone completely. This journey of life is a search for truth. This journey of faith is following you – every step of the way – thru the joy of every pain, right here in this moment.*

*AMEN.*

Here is another incident that happened as a result of journaling on March 10, 2008. In the month of March I was planning a seminar for women called, "Calling All Women to Prosper in the Workplace." I was to give that seminar on May 31, 2008, which was a Saturday.

In my journal, I asked for affirmation from my Heavenly Father to encourage me to speak at the seminar. I wanted to know that this is what He wanted me to do. Was this God's will or mine? I want to be sure I was on the right path.

On Friday night, May 30, 2008, the night before the seminar, I told my husband I needed to get out of the house, that I was ready for the seminar, and just needed to get my mind off of it for a while. I suggested we go to the bookstore.

On the way to the bookstore, Tim asked me if I had a particular book in mind and my response was, "I guess if I am going to publicly speak, I should find a book on that. I have no author; I have no title." So when we arrived at the bookstore, I went to the service desk and asked for a book on public speaking.

The clerk walked me over to the section and she pulled out one book from the bottom shelf. I saw that it had a white cover and she handed it to me, "We have this one," she said. I looked at the title and almost fell to the floor. The title was, "Talk Like Jesus – Change Your World with the S. I. M. P. L. E. Steps of the Master Communicator" by Lynn Wilford Scarborough. I told the clerk, "Stop. This is exactly the book I was looking for."

Is that a coincidence? I don't think so. I call that a "GOD incident." The words on the front cover said, "Apply the lessons of the most effective speaker of all time to your life and career." Yes, that is exactly the book I need to read because I want to model my life after Jesus Christ.

I walked over to my husband in the bookstore with the biggest grin. I couldn't even speak. I just held up the book so he could read it. I was in shock! He said to me, "That is so amazing!" *Amen!* (As I sit here writing this story, tears are welling up in my eyes. Our God is so incredible.)

To me that meant God was saying, "Yes, go my daughter. Follow the steps that Jesus used when He spoke and changed lives on this planet. Go ye therefore." Amen.

These are just a couple of examples of how journaling has affected my life. I started journaling when I knew that my life was empty and dissatisfying and I wanted more. I didn't know how to find the answers or who I was, but through the power of journaling and developing my relationship with God, I was making huge strides in my discovery journey.

I learned how to express myself through journaling. It has been an amazing experience. I journaled for more than 10 years and then at the age of 50, I knew that I no longer wanted to be a CPA in the business world, sitting behind a desk from 8 a.m. – 5 p.m.

Remember, earlier I said, "I knew that at age 50 I wanted to do something else. During my 40s, I would tell my friends, 'at age 50 I want to do something else. I am not sure what that is yet, but I want to do something else besides CPA work. I want to do something totally different, something totally unique.'"

On September 16, 2008, seven months after being laid off from work as a VP of Finance from a government contractor, I turned 50 years old. I guess speaking the words out loud put the wheels in motion, and the doors were opened for me at age 50.

Life by Design had been in the works since 2006, two years before. Now I could give my full attention to this business and do what I believe God was and is calling me to do: coach women to live their life on purpose, and speak at events about living a life of purpose. I was getting the chance to make an impact on people's lives in a unique and powerful way.

I recently attended a training workshop and the teacher said this, "All growth happens when you are alone! You face up to the truth." Journaling is spending time alone and writing it down makes it *real*.

I hope this chapter has encouraged you to journal. Begin with five minutes a day and see if this does not make a difference in your life. Listen. Be honest with yourself. Have fun!

# Creative Connection – You Are an Artist!

Whenever I think of an artist, or hear the word artist, I think of a woman dressed in black, behaving eccentrically, wearing a lot of jewelry, and painting a wild picture. I never thought of myself as an artist. As a child I would entertain myself for hours playing with paper, glitter, and crayons. That was my earliest connection to being creative.

What was it like for you when you were growing up? Did you get the chance to paint? Did you take piano lessons? Did you write your own short stories? Did someone encourage your artistic talent?

When my mother was in her teens, she wanted to be an artist. She ordered a painting kit from a company in New York City. When the package arrived, she was thrilled. However, her father made her send it back and told her it was foolish to want to be an artist. My mom was heartbroken.

After my mom was married and started to have children, the desire to paint was still there and she began dabbling in water color. It was in her early 70s when she actually got serious about art lessons and picked up water color painting again. She was good at it! She was excited! Her passion was to paint flowers! When I would visit her, she would proudly show off her latest creation.

I made a comment about how good it was and asked her to show me how it was done. She did a demonstration and I said it looked like fun. For Christmas that year a package arrived from my mom on my doorstep.

Inside that package was water color brushes, paints, and a palette. How fabulous! I began to search for a local teacher and lessons that met my schedule.

Not long after, my husband and I attended an artist's showing. The artist's name was Payge Semmes and her artwork was on display at a local university. I noticed that some of her paintings were water color and asked if she would give me one-on-one lessons. She agreed! Payge and I started meeting together on a regular basis. She would show me how to paint the object and then I would try using the same technique she did.

I knew my paintings were not works of "art," but I was having a blast giving it my best effort. Time flew by when I was working on a painting. Soon after, I attended an arts and crafts festival in Huntsville, Alabama and came across a demonstration of five local artists. They were working on the same painting. Each one would work on the painting for 15 minutes and then hand it off to the next painter. It was interesting as I stood there mesmerized watching them paint so easily. I ended up buying the painting at the end of the Art Festival and it still hangs in my art studio today.

One of those five painters was teaching classes at the local art supply store and he told me that I was welcome to join them every other Thursday night. So I joined the group of artists on a regular basis.

When we came to class, each one showed up with a picture that we were working on. The art teacher would go from painting to painting and offer suggestions on how to make it better. By listening to his critiques, comments and suggestions, I was learning. I did this for several years. My painting focused on general buildings. Then my subjects became houses. Then I started painting pictures of friend's houses and giving the portraits away as gifts. Then others began asking me if I would do paintings of their homes – a commissioned painting – you bet! I started selling my paintings. What a great feeling knowing that people appreciated my art work! This was a process of about four years.

Here is one of my most recent paintings:

This painting is Shannon's House of Compassion located in Huntsville, Alabama. It is located across the street from the hospital. Shannon's House is available for families who have loved ones in the hospital that need to stay for long periods of time, but cannot afford hotels or places to stay. They can stay at Shannon's House for free.

## My Awakening

Because of my awakening, that I too am an artist, I developed the "Creative Connection Workshop" for women to help *them* discover *their* unique creativity. One of the things we discuss in the workshop are creative affirmations. They are as follows:

## Creative Affirmations

1. I AM unique.
2. I will honor my uniqueness by getting quiet, journaling, and taking long walks to listen to what my Creator wants to reveal to me.
3. I AM creative.
4. I will give myself permission to play.
5. I will give myself permission to take an inspirational class to fuel my creativity.
6. I will acknowledge that fueling my creativity is not selfish, BUT necessary.
7. I AM an artist.
8. I will use my senses; sight, smell, and listening to nurture my creativity, because beauty is all around me.
9. I will bring joy to others by sharing my creativity.
10. My creativity gives me purpose and peace.
11. My Creator has designed me to create. I cannot NOT create.
12. I will buy a piece of jewelry, an apron, or piece of clothing that speaks to my authentic, creative self, and wear it to remind myself who I am.
13. I am willing to share or teach my creative talent to a child or friend.
14. I will use my creativity in a volunteer organization.
15. I will continue to look for new ways to express my creativity.
16. I add value as a woman because I have something to share.
17. The best way to find myself is to lose myself in a creative project.
18. I will be open to learn new things.
19. I will find a special, creative place in my home that will be set aside for me to be creative.
20. God has a plan for my creative ability and it is good!

I love all of these affirmations. It would be hard to pick out just one of which to focus. However, "My Creator has designed me to create; I cannot NOT create" really speaks to me. Which one of these 20 affirmations really speaks to your heart and soul? Circle the one you like best.

During this workshop, I give the women permission to play again. They go through magazines and pull out any picture, color, or words that speak to their soul. Then at the end of an hour they take their magazine clippings and glue them onto a piece of newspaper creating a poster. Together, while looking at the poster, we, as a group try to make sense of that poster and tell the originator our observations about their creativity.

One of my participant's in the workshop wrote, "I don't consider myself creative, but I found out that is not true. You can take something you enjoy and take it to another level." This particular participant discovered she loved plants and gardening; but not only that, she discovered she wanted to create a tranquility garden. This particular woman is in college to get her degree in psychology and wants to open a home for abused women. Wouldn't a tranquility garden be awesome at a home for abused women? I envision the women that live there pitching in and taking care of the tranquility garden. How healing is that!

Another one of the women attending the workshop discovered that words inspired her. She had a love for words. Her poster was plastered with words. She wrote, "I would say that I learned an amazing way to begin to learn about myself and other interests I had. Creativity is relaxing, but [it also] helps maintain knowledge of myself."

The following is an excerpt taken straight from "Simple Abundance, a Daybook of Comfort and Joy" written by Sarah Ban Breathnach.

*"Start thinking of yourself as an artist and your life as a work in progress. Works in progress are never perfect. But changes can be made to the rough draft during rewrites. Another color can be added to the canvas. The film can be tightened during editing. Art evolves. So does life. Art is never stagnant. Neither is life. The beautiful, authentic life you are creating for yourself and those you love is your art. It is the highest art. You are like no other being ever created since the beginning of time; you are incomparable."*

You are like no other being ever created; you are incomparable – *Wow!*

I have put together 12 Creative Exercises to inspire you to find out more about your creativity, more about who you are, and more about what truly speaks to your heart and soul.

## Creative Exercises: A Time to Discover

Do you know what speaks to your soul? Do you know what energizes you? Would you like to know more about yourself? One way to discover who you are is to go on a discovery journey – a creative exercise. Give yourself permission to spend a couple of hours a month seeking and finding the woman that has been created. Find out what resonates with you. Find out what speaks to your heart and soul.

A creative exercise is not an original idea. I came across the idea while reading "Simple Abundance." A creative exercise is something to do by yourself – *just you* – to discover what makes *you* sing; to discover what speaks to *your* heart; to discover what speaks to *your* soul. It is important to go by yourself so you are not influenced by your friends. This is not about what speaks to your friends. It is about what speaks to *you*.

Every woman should find out who they are, what makes them unique, and what is their creative gifting? Every women needs time out, time alone— to do something to recharge their soul. Invest in yourself. This is necessary! Those of us that are familiar with Bible stories know that even Jesus had to get away and be alone. There was only so much He could do and He was perfect! He had to regain His strength in order to continue doing His ministry.

Ban Breathnach says, "When you embark on creative exercises, your authentic self will lovingly reveal to you the beautiful mystery that is *you*. Realize that nurturing your imaginations and developing a relationship with your authentic self is an *investment* that you can no longer put on the back burner. Expect nothing less than signs and wonders to follow."

On that note, the following is a collection of creative exercises that will enlighten *you* and inspire *you* to spend time alone "nurturing your imaginations and developing that relationship with your authentic self."

The purpose is to give you ideas that are either free or very inexpensive. Give yourself permission to take time to discover, to journey, to smile, to dream, to laugh, and to *have fun*!

## Strolling through an antique mall

Antique malls are great for discovering all kinds of treasures. Roam the aisles slowly one way, then turn around and roam the aisles again in the opposite direction so you can check out what's on both sides of the row. It is amazing what you will spot when you walk the aisles in both directions. Antique malls offer a variety of booths with different objects, such as: table linens, fabrics, jewelry, books, lamps, furniture, artwork, dishes, quilts, etc. Look around and just listen to your heart.

What memories come back to you as you roam the aisles? Is there something that reminds you of your childhood, or reminds you of your grandmother, your mother – a piece of jewelry, a piece of furniture, a board game, a dish?

Do you like to recycle old things? Do you see an object you can repurpose, meaning to use in a different manner than what it was originally intended?

Remember, you are on a discovery to find your "authentic self" – what speaks to you today? What catches your eye? Why does it catch your eye? Is it the subject matter? Is it the particular color? Is it a particular style that appeals to you?

For me, I collect antique cotton table clothes. The pale shades of blue really speak to my heart. If the cloth has holes, I repurpose it by making pillows out of them. Most of them are in pretty good shape and I use them on my kitchen table or on my outdoor picnic table. Another thing I like to look for are small pieces of furniture that can be painted in pretty pastel colors and used as porch furniture.

Write down your memories, your thoughts, your connections to your childhood, or take notes of a particular object that you may be interested in buying. You may not be able to afford it today; however, it could become a reality through a birthday gift or Christmas gift.

## Discovering your decorating style

Walking into a well-designed home décor store really speaks to my spirit. It is relaxing, tranquil, and smells wonderful. It just puts me in a place of peacefulness. The items on display often include: bedding, candles, towels, lamps, pottery, dishes, and fabrics. I want it all!

This creative exercise is about discovering and defining your decorating style. Do you know your decorating style? Is it casual, shabby chic, contemporary, traditional, eclectic? Do you like old things or new things?

Visit home décor stores. Visit furniture stores. Start a picture journal of home décor. Look at home décor magazines and cut out pictures you are drawn to and glue them in your picture journal. Pick up sample color swatches from the home improvement store. Write down notes in your journal about your style; modern, cottage, traditional. What scent or fragrance appeals to you; floral, musk, fruity?

Have a conversation with the sales clerk while engaging in your creative exercises. They will be able to help you identify your style. Go home and take a critical eye toward your own home. Your home should be your haven. Is it comfortable? Does it resonate with your style today? Does it smell wonderful? Your home should reflect you!

What do your guests see as they step through the front door and into your home? This is their first impression of *you*. No matter the size of your home, it can be beautiful and can reflect your "authentic self." My sister walked into my home and commented that it was "homey." This means a lot to me because I want my guests to feel at home as soon as they walk in.

## Finding just the right pen

I don't know about you, but I need to write things down. I would rather use a day planner, than an electronic gadget to keep my calendar. There are certain pens that feel better in my hand. My penmanship looks better when I have "just the right pen."

This creative exercise is about visiting office supply stores and craft supply stores. Try out different pens. Write with them at the store. In the scrapbooking department of a craft supply store, you will find gel pens in all different colors, including metallic gold and silver. The metallic pens are my favorite. I write in a journal with the gold metallic pen and the page comes to life; it shimmers and glows – it makes my words come to life.

Pens come in all shapes and sizes and are made from different materials. I have a friend who collects pens made from wood and from bone. I know another woman, a CPA, who uses a pink pen for reviewing the accounting staff's work in her office. That is her trademark – a pink pen.

For work, I like the thinner pens with blue ink. It looks cleaner to me and my penmanship is acceptable. I cannot write with a fatter pen. For play, it is the shimmering gold gel pen. For an inexpensive fee, you can even order pens with your name engraved on them. If you ordered pens, what would you put on the pen to radiate your authentic self? What would it say?

During this creative exercise, take your time to find "just the right pen." You may find one for work and you may find one for play. I sure hope so!

## Thumbing through magazines

Perhaps you have old magazines lying around the house. If not, you can go to yard sales and buy magazines very inexpensively or ask your friends for theirs once they have finished reading. Or maybe you enjoy visiting your local bookstore, grabbing a cup of coffee, and glancing through the magazine section. This is a good place to begin because their choices are varied. Which do you gravitate toward?

Magazines offer topics of all ranges: hobbies, architecture, business, home décor, travel, fashion, etc.

This creative exercise is designed to see what catches your eye. Listen to your heart. This is done by tearing out pages from your magazines. Tear out the page that speaks to you. As you tear out pages, do you see a theme? Is it a color that resonates with you? Is it a style? Is it a place? Is it architecture or gardening?

Here is what happened to me as I was thumbing through magazines. Beach scenes and beach colors kept speaking to me. My conclusion, I wanted a beach house! That is what really spoke to me. I took the pages that I had torn out of the magazines, cut the pictures out in different shapes and sizes, and created a dream poster. When finished, I placed this poster in my office at work. *One day,* I would own a beach house. That dream poster became a reality 13 months later in March 1999 and my husband and I became proud owners of a beach house for 10 years. Learn more about this in the chapter entitled, **10 Steps to Living Life on Purpose**.

Perhaps you want to make your own dream poster or picture journal? What is your authentic self saying to you during this exercise?

## Creating an Adult Toy Box

When was the last time you played a game, rode a bicycle, swung on a swing, or colored in a coloring book? These are things children do to play.

We cannot forget the power of play and how to have fun. My mother who is now retired says, "Fun is at the top of my list!" This creative exercise is to build your own toy box, to allow you to connect to your inner child. So here are some ideas:

First, you need a box or an empty drawer. You can take a shoe box and decorate it with wrapping paper or fabric. If you create your own box, you can use stickers, buttons, or ribbons, to dress it up and make it "authentically yours." Be original. Have fun. This is another way for your uniqueness to shine.

Now go on your creative exercise and take $10 to shop at your favorite dollar store, office supply store, or stationery / gift shop. What do you see? Cool colored pens, pencils, erasers, stickers, paper clips, or crayons? What about funny cards?

Is there a cartoon strip that makes you laugh or a comic book? Place it in your toy box. Is there a certain kind of candy you ate as a child? What about a child's book that you love to read? Buy a box of crayons, stickers, paper, craft scissors, or cut outs and put it in your box.

What were some of your favorite toys as a child? Marbles, cards, jacks? Maybe you have stray parts around the house to a board game, such as monopoly or scrabble, and can put the pieces from the board game in your box. Scrabble pieces remind me of time spent with my grandmother playing for hours.

Creating an adult toy box is not an original idea. I came across this idea in the book "Simple Abundance." The purpose of the adult toy box is to remind you to have fun. Stop. Take time out and play. I would even recommend taking your toy box to work. When you are having a bad day, reach for your toy box, look through it, do something during a quick break or during lunch. Your toy box is supposed to make you smile, laugh, and feel young again. I have a friend who has kept encouraging notes from others. The notes make her smile and they lift her spirits when she reads them. Whatever is in your toy box, *know this*: you are never too old to play.

# Stroll through a garden or park

I love to be surrounded by beauty and nature. My husband is the one who has put time in our yard and we are finally reaping the benefits. Our yard looks beautiful. I know I am older now because I like to be still in the yard and listen to the birds sing and to the sound of the wind chimes. Time alone, in the quiet, can calm my spirit.

During this creative exercise, I encourage you to walk through a public park and take a seat on a park bench. Maybe there is a bench by a fountain. Be still. Get quiet. Listen to your heart. What is your heart telling you? Write notes (using "just the right pen") to remember what you are learning and discovering as you sit quietly or take a camera and take photos of the things you see. A close up of a flower or an interesting rock wall. You get the picture!

If you have access and money for a trip to a botanical garden, this is also a relaxing venue. Perhaps you are a gardener and walking through this garden inspires you to work in your yard. Take notes of which plants you like and make a trip to your local nursery. Some nurseries are set up with a path of shrubs and bushes laid to mimic an actual garden. This way you can see how the plants work in a garden environment. We have a local nursery that is set up as a small botanical garden and soft music plays in the background.

Perhaps you have never planted anything before, but you have an interest. Visit a nursery and start with a potted plant. Start with something simple, like a house plant. Talk with the gardeners at the nursery. Ask questions. They are the experts and they love to share their knowledge. Take time to learn. In our town, we have a botanical garden that offers classes so that you can become a master gardener.

Fresh flowers in your home will bring color and fragrance. They will be sure to cheer you up as well as everyone else in the home. Fresh flowers can be found in your local grocery store and are very inexpensive. Which flower will you choose? I like potted plants because they last longer and can be moved from room to room. What is your "authentic self" telling you about flowers and plants?

# Planning a dream vacation

If you could go anywhere on a vacation and money was not holding you back, where would you go?

Have you ever watched a movie and thought you needed to visit the featured location? For me, that movie is "Sound of Music." It is one of my favorite films. I would love to visit Austria because of the beautiful mountains and architecture.

What do you enjoy doing on vacation? Do you like to lounge and read? Do you like to visit historical places? Do you enjoy physical activities like riding a bicycle or hiking? Do you prefer the mountains or the beach? Do you enjoy a place that is secluded or do you want to be part of a tour group and have the opportunity to meet other people from around the country? Answering these questions gives you a better glimpse of the true you and where you would like to travel and what you would like to do.

Have you ever thought about going on a cruise? Take your creative exercise on the internet. Print out pages of places to see, things to do. Start a file folder called "Dream Vacation." Think about why you want to go? What is it about this place that speaks to your soul? Maybe you want to make another dream poster for that dream vacation.

# Cooking as ART: Creative Discoveries in the Kitchen

Do you prefer to bake or cook? Have you bought a new cookbook lately? Are you addicted to a favorite cooking show on TV?

During this creative exercise, I invite you to try out a new recipe. Ask yourself, what am I hungry for? What is my comfort food? If you do not have a cookbook available, go on the internet and "Google" the recipe.

I encourage you to try out a new spice, a new flavor. Have you ever used fresh herbs? Do you want to cook your grandmother's apple pie recipe and fill your home with delightful scents that take you back in time?

Jacqueline Deval tells us in her book, "Reckless Appetites: A Culinary Romance" ... "you can never re-create the past. But you can shape your own future. And you can make a cake."

I hear a chocolate cake with chocolate fudge frosting calling my name. Yum!

Bon Appetite!

## Find Your Authentic Fashion Style

Did you ever own an outfit that when you put it on, you felt like a million dollars? In fact, you felt like you could conquer the world in that outfit! That outfit gave you confidence. When was the last time you read a book or did research on what outfit would look best on your body type?

"Dress Your Best - The Complete Guide to Finding the Style That's Right for Your Body" by Stacy London and Clinton Kelly helps you figure out what body shape you have and how to dress for that body shape. It gives illustrations, with outfits for your body type, an outfit for work, an outfit for the evening, and a casual outfit.

Today, your creative exercise is to go shopping and try on outfits that suit your body style. I want to suggest classic, quality clothes that will last a long time. In addition to your local department store, try an upscale consignment shop. You could spend $100 for a good fitting pair of black pants and wear them over and over, say 100 times, it may end up only costing you $1.00 per outfit by the time it is all said and done.

This creative exercise is not about spending lots of money or "shopping therapy," but to focus on what looks best on you, and finding the style that suits your personality and body type.

Hold colors up to your face. Does a pale pink, dark emerald green, white, or gold brighten your face? There are certain colors that will look better on you based on your skin tone.  Remember to look for the book called "Color Me Beautiful" by Carole Jackson.

What about accessories? Fashion accessories are the finishing touches that define us.  For me, personally, I have started collecting brooches from the antique malls and wear them with my suits.  I want a brooch to be my trademark.  For my mom, who sports short hair, long dangling earrings are her trademark.

I want you to look and feel young again.  I want you to hold your head high because you feel like a million dollars.  I want your spirit to sing! A friend told me my style was "classic with an edge."  So, what does your authentic style reflect about you?

## Writing In a Journal

Take the first step and buy a journal.  Find one that is really pretty or buy one that has a simple cover and decorate it with ribbons, buttons, or fabric. Make it your own!

Develop quiet time. Is there such a thing?  As I mentioned previously, the dishwasher should not be going and neither should the washing machine. You should try to be alone in the still of the morning or the still of the night with your journal in front of you.

What are you thinking about today?  What comes to mind?  Are you frustrated?  Are you grateful?  Are you goal setting?  Are you discouraged? Whatever is in your head, write it down in your journal.

Take time to discover your innermost thoughts.  Allow your Heavenly Father to speak to you through your journal.  This is an amazing exercise! Write, "Father, what do you want to teach me today?" and then let the first thoughts that come to your mind flow onto the paper.  Let the answer reveal itself to you on paper.

Try writing in your journal for at least five minutes to start. Do this creative exercise more than once. Try it again and again. As you write, do you see a theme? Is there something that stays on your heart and your mind? Should you pursue this thought?

After journaling for 6 months, go back over your journal and read what you have written. It is validating to see down the road how things have worked out, how goals are obtained, how troubles don't seem to be such a big deal anymore. What is your innermost self revealing to you through your journal writing?

## 20 Wishes

When you wish upon a star ...

When was the last time you made a wish? Don't be fooled by thinking wishes are just for children. A *wish* is telling your head what your heart wants to do. A wish is like feeding your spirit. It is your spirit that brings you life. Make a list of 20 wishes for living.

Often times, as women, we feel obligated to take care of everybody else and not ourselves. While taking care of everyone else, we forget who we are supposed to be, we get lost, we settle. We stop exercising and gain weight. We stop taking care of our appearance. We stop buying clothes for ourselves and wear clothes that are worn out or no longer fit. We are emotionally exhausted and frustrated.

This creative exercise is devised to awaken your heart and awaken your soul. Take time on this creative exercise to write down 20 wishes now. It may take a while to come up with 20, but it will be worth it, and they will be yours. I came up with this creative exercise after reading Debbie Macomber's book called "Twenty Wishes."

# Class for FUN!

When was the last time you took a class for fun? Have you looked at your local newspaper lately? Do you have a community college that is offering classes? Have you researched online for a class in the community? There are so many classes from which to choose.

This creative exercise is about looking through the newspaper, community college listing, or online and reading about the different classes that are being offered. What class is your local art gallery offering? What peaks your interest? Watercolor painting? Computer Class? Quilting? Home Improvement? Learning another language? Cooking?

How much does it cost? If cash flow is an issue, can you exchange your time to help during the class as a host instead of actually paying for the class? That is a win, win situation for both you and the instructor – earn to learn. Or can you bring several paying friends with you so that the instructor will allow you to attend free of charge? Can you audit the class?

When I was coaching, one of my clients was assigned this task! She was to spend the next two weeks looking through the newspaper to see what classes were out there. She did not have to register for the class. She just had to investigate. When we met together again, I asked her if she had found a class that piqued her interest and she started laughing and blushing. She said, "Not only did a find a class, but I enrolled, and am now taking belly dancing lessons." She was thrilled! This class was giving her a chance to express herself in a way she never knew possible. It was a sense of freedom for her.

Investigate and listen to what your heart is whispering as it is telling you what to do.

## SUMMARY

If you want to continue this creative journey, I recommend "The Path" by Laurie Beth Jones. She encourages you to write your own mission statement for work and life and to take that mission statement to the next level by creating a vision for yourself. It is a great book for further self discovery.

You are unique. Finding your gifts, your uniqueness, and using it in an environment where you can get paid is like "hitting a home run." You hear the smack of the ball as it hits the bat and everyone in the stand starts to cheer. You are laughing in elation as you run the bases with your hands raised high over your head. You can take your time as you run the bases because you realize no one can knock you out of the game. You are in the spotlight. You are encouraged by the masses to keep on running. You cross home plate lighthearted and smiling. This feels good. This feels right. You are exactly where you should be. And being in a place where you are meant to be is a place of joy, contentment, and knowing that this is right. This is a life of abundance!

Your creator has made you with a uniqueness. Have you found it? Have you hit that home run yet? If so, I applaud you. If not, I would encourage you to start your discovery journey, like myself. If you are stuck, try a creative exercise or consider hiring a life coach to help you move forward.

Have Fun! *Enjoy* and listen. Your true self is speaking softly.

You don't have to be a woman dressed in black, acting eccentric, wearing a lot of jewelry, and painting a wild painting to be an artist. Each of us is an artist. An artist is someone who listens with her heart and follows it, she possesses the ability to listen – to hear that inner voice and she follows her passion to create. Expressing our creativity can take many forms; you are an artist as you try out that new recipe, as you take a computer class, as you try creative ideas in the workplace to sell your products, as you sit and write a poem in your journal.

*You are an artist!* Start thinking of yourself as an artist. You add beauty to this world with your unique way of expressing yourself and your creativity. This world needs you and your creativity.

# 10 steps to Living Life on Purpose

Let me begin by telling you a story about Jack. It is Sunday afternoon and Jack is reading the business section of the newspaper. He puts the newspaper down in frustration and says to his wife, "I dread going to work tomorrow. No one appreciates what I do. There is nothing happening in the office. I hate my job."

Monday morning rolls around and Jack is 30 minutes late. He arrives in his office, turns on the computer, grabs his coffee cup, and heads to the break room.

In the breakroom, the coffee pot has just enough coffee for his cup and he says to himself, "I'm not making coffee. That is not my job." He pours his coffee, turns off the coffee pot and heads back to his office.

His computer is now on and he brings up the internet. He begins to check out the news and see what is happening in the world. Forty-five minutes later, Sam walks into his office and announces, "Have you heard? Tom just got promoted." With disgust, he continues, "and he hasn't even been here for one year. He is now going to be the program manager on the new contract." Sam leaves the room.

Jack is now angry. He says out loud, "I always get looked over. This is so unfair."

Now, let me tell you about Diane. It is Sunday afternoon and Diane is reading the business section of the newspaper. She circles an advertisement about a Lunch and Learn coming up next week that she would like to attend. She circles another class that is being offered at the local university that would help improve her skills at the office.

She puts the newspaper down and says to her husband, "I am having the best time at work. We are coming up with some creative ideas for marketing. I feel like I am adding value. I love my job."

Monday morning rolls around and Diane is 30 minutes early. She arrives in her office, turns on the computer, grabs her coffee cup, and heads to the break room.

In the break room the coffee pot has just enough coffee for her cup and she says to herself, "I think I will make a fresh pot of coffee." While the pot is brewing, she picks up a towel and begins to wipe down the counter that is splattered with coffee and sugar. She pours her coffee and heads back to her office.

Her computer is now on and she brings up her calendar. She looks over her day and makes notes about the classes that she circled in the paper yesterday. She signs up for the Lunch and Learn and the class at the local university.

Forty-five minutes later Sam walks into her office and announces, "Have you heard? Tom just got promoted." With disgust, he continues "and he hasn't even been here for one year. He is now going to be the program manager on the new contract." Sam leaves the room.

Diane gets up from her desk and walks down to Tom's office. She says to Tom, "Congratulations on the promotion. By the way, I am really good with numbers, budgets, and forecasts. If you need help with this contract, I will be more than happy to help."

Diane walks back to her office.

End of story.

In this example, who is living by default? Jack. Jack doesn't take any action. Jack is not purposely taking charge of his life. Jack is allowing life to happen to him. Jack is settling. Jack does not volunteer to help with either making coffee or with the new contract. Instead, he sits back and says, "Woe is me."

Diane, on the other hand, has a whole different attitude. Diane is about taking action. Diane knows who she is and what she does well in the office. She is willing to share that and use it for the company's benefit. Diane goes above and beyond the call of duty and makes the pot of coffee without being asked. Diane is improving her skills by attending classes. Diane enjoys her job and it shows. Diane is living on purpose.

*(For this chapter I would recommend having a journal and a pen nearby. You will be asked lots of "laser" questions that need some attention and thought.)*

I have developed 10 steps to become more enthusiastic about who you are; more enthusiastic about finding your passion; and more enthusiastic about how you can use your talents and abilities to give back to your work, your community, or your home environment.

1. **Take Inventory.**
   Make a list of your strengths. Be honest with yourself, this is not the time to be timid.

   For example, your list may look like: I work well with people. I am organized. I understand numbers and financial reports. I have good leadership skills.

   Think about a time you worked on a project that just flowed. Before you knew it, it was time for lunch. The day just flew by. This project came to you naturally. What were you doing? What attributes were you using during this project?

My strengths include:

_____

_____

_____

_____

_____

_____

In the story above, Diane knew what her strengths were and was more than willing to share these in the workplace.

After you list your strengths, can you take one of these strengths and add it to your current job description? For example, when I was a VP of Finance, the thought came to me that I wanted to give our employees something more than just a paycheck. I thought about Dave Ramsey's "Financial Peace" class. I called to find out how much Dave Ramsey's group charged to teach employees and it was way more than we were willing to pay. So, I thought, "Why couldn't I teach this class?"

I did. I developed a class for employees called "Way to Wealth." After several employees attended the class, word spread. Employees began to approach me and wanted to know when I was going to teach the next class. I was really encouraged when one of the employees came up to me and said with a big smile, "I started my emergency fund."

Teaching "Way to Wealth" was not a part of my job description, but I made it happen. I was using my gifting and adding value

to the company as well. Teaching the employees really ener-
gized me because I felt like I was making a difference in their
lives.

Is there something you can add to your job description that you
are not currently doing, but you are passionate about it and you
think it would add value to the company? If not at work, is there a
strength you wish to bring to your church or community that would
add value?

I will add value by taking the following strength into the world:

_____

_____

_____

_____

_____

_____

Continuing with the idea of taking inventory, not only do you need
to think of your strengths, but you *must* make a list of your weaknesses. What drains you?

Your list may consist of: I can't sit at a desk from 8 a.m. – 5 p.m. every
day. Speaking in front of people or facilitating a meeting makes me
sick to my stomach. I am not a good communicator.

Be honest with yourself and take note of these things as well.

My weaknesses include:

_____

_____

_____

_____

_____

_____

It is important to know what your weaknesses are so that you will know what does not work for you. Let's say, for instance, someone approaches you about a job and tells you what it pays. I don't want the pay to be the determining factor as to whether or not you should accept employment. Let me explain.

Let's say when you start thinking about the job description, you get this knot in your stomach and you know this is not the right job for you. That knot in your stomach is your body telling you it is not the right job for you.

If you take the job for the money, you will not add value to the position. You will be miserable and you will not do the task well. This will affect your overall reputation.

By the way, those things that drain you, think about delegating those tasks. Is there someone at work who can help you with those tasks? The same can be done at home. Is there someone at home you can delegate to who can help with your "to do" list? Can you hire someone part time to do those tasks that drain you? Can you hire a college student that is looking for experience? I have a friend who sells Mary Kay products and is a dynamic Mary Kay consultant. She does not desire to sit at the computer and do paperwork – that drains her and she knows it. She has hired a part-time person to do that for her.

Your weakness may be someone else's strength. That becomes a WIN/WIN situation. Hire that person or delegate the work that drains you to the person who loves to do it.

If you are unemployed right now and were recently laid off, this is a good time to take inventory. After analyzing your strengths, look around and see what is in your home. What do you have to work with? Is it a computer? Is it a sewing machine? Or is it wood working equipment? Take your strengths and volunteer so people can see who you are, see your credibility, as well as witness your work ethic. They just might hire you full time doing what you love to do.

When you use your true, natural gifts in the workplace and get paid for doing it, it is like hitting a home run. At the end of the day, you can say, "This feels good. This feels right. I had the best day." That is what I call "Living on Purpose" and not by default.

2. **Be quiet. Be still.**
   I spend quiet time writing in a journal. This journal contains my dreams, my thoughts, phrases, inspirational words, etc. I will even ask myself questions in my journal. After asking the question, I will be still and wait for the answer. The question might be, "What is the right next step for me?"

When I am quiet and still, the answer will come and identify what I need to do next, who I need to call, what marketing material I need to pull together, and who to call to help me with that marketing material. This very thing happened to me a few years back while I still owned my CPA practice. One Sunday afternoon, I was quietly sitting still thinking about my business, when the thought came to me that I needed to touch base with a certain individual. When I called that person the next day, who was the owner of an optometry business, she told me she just lost her CPA and was looking for another. We made an appointment for that week and I was hired as her new CPA. Here is an example of questions that I encourage you to ask yourself and answer:

Is there currently a goal I am working on?  What is that goal?  When do I want to complete that goal?

_____

_____

_____

_____

_____

What is NOT working for me?  What am I frustrated with?

_____

_____

_____

_____

_____

If I could change one thing, what would that be?

_____

_____

_____

_____

_____

I love asking myself these questions because they open up my heart and my mind to my Creator who loves me and wants the best for me. By answering these questions, it builds confidence and gives me honesty about who I am.

When you write down the answers to these questions, do not be surprised if the people you need to meet to make your dreams come to fruition, begin to enter your life. Or, that someone will say something that you need to hear. Perhaps a book will fall off the book shelf that you need to read. That is the "magic" behind journaling. I call it "magic," but really it is the manifestation of what you are thinking about. You are more aware of what you are asking and seeking.

Go back and review the chapter on "The Power of Journaling."

3. **Invest in yourself.**
   Never stop learning. If you need to obtain certification to become more credible in your position, get certified.

   Keep reading. Keep listening to CDs. Keep attending workshops and seminars that will develop you as a person or expand your skill set in your career. In the story above, Diane read about a Lunch and

Learn and a class that was being offered at a local college. She then took action and registered.

Take a fun class. Learn a new language. Learn how to paint or how to draw. Learn how to play the piano.

In the back of this book, there are recommendations of books that have been helpful to me to grow as an individual. Visit a book store and walk the aisles. See what books peak your interest.

Keep asking questions. Grow. Stretch. Keep your mind active. You may also meet some fun, interesting  people along the way that share your same interests.

**4.   Set Priorities.**
List your personal priorities and list your professional priorities.

My top five personal priorities are:

_____

_____

_____

_____

_____

My top five professional priorities are:

_____

_____

_____

_____

_____

What do you value?  What is important to you?

_____

_____

_____

_____

_____

Whatever is important to you, this is where you will spend your time and your money.

I know someone who says, "show me your checkbook and your calendar, and I will tell you what  is important to you."

As for your time, you only have 24 hours in one day.  When an opportunity is presented to you, rather than giving an immediate "yes," allow yourself time to think about it.   Ask yourself, is this a good fit for me? Does this fit into my priorities? For instance, if one of your priorities is to spend more time with your family and this opportunity will pull you away from your family, then the answer is simple.  You just say "*no.*"

## 5. Control Cash Flow.

If I were to ask you right now, how much do you spend on groceries per month, do you know the answer? Is it $500, $600, $800? Just for giggles, write down in the margin of this book what you think you spend on groceries per month.

This next exercise is an eye opener. What I want you to do is track your expenses for 30 days. Use your debit card to record every transaction for the month. See my Excel spreadsheet, **Where is My Money Going?** in the appendix to use as a template to track your expenses.

If you write a check, list that on the spreadsheet as well. Include your credit card transactions on the spreadsheet. You will notice that the spreadsheet is set up with categories. The goal is to track how you are spending your money now! Again, this will be an eye opener in the sense that you will be shocked how much money you are spending and where you are spending it.

Once you know the total amount you are spending each month, compare that to the amount that you are paid each month. Is it less than what you are bringing in? Or is it more? If the expenses are more than what you are bringing in, this is not good and you are NOT in control of your spending.

You cannot live on purpose if you are worried about cash flow. You cannot live on purpose when you are not able to pay your bills. You are probably overwhelmed and distracted. This is an exercise that will put you in control of how you spend your money.

By going through this exercise, you will actually see how much you spend on groceries. Now, go look at the number you wrote in the margin earlier in this chapter. How does it compare? Were you close?

You CAN come up with a plan to cut back and use the excess to pay down debt or other obligations. For instance, if you decide that $200 each paycheck should be used to buy groceries, then you put $200 in an envelope for groceries and only use that money set aside. That is the Dave Ramsey method. My rule of thumb; the number of people in household X $50 per week. So if you have a household of four people, that would be 4 X $50 = $200 per week on groceries – I am talking food only, not paper products, cleaning products, or other consumables.

Before going to the grocery store, make a menu for the week. This does not take long and you usually know your family's favorites. Compare your menu to what you already have in the pantry and the refrigerator; now make your grocery list. When you go to the grocery store, only buy what is on your list!

Speaking of your pantry, I bet you could live out of your pantry for 30 days. Look in your pantry and identify what you can use to make a meal without even going to the grocery store. How many boxes of cereal do you have? Can you eat cereal for dinner one night? When you come up with a dollar amount per week that you want to spend on groceries, this is called taking "Control!" I will spend $200 per week on groceries, period!

This is just one example of how you can be in control of how you spend your money and not allowing your money to control you. You decide how your money will be spent. You will also notice that once you start paying in cash, you really start thinking, "do I really need this?" This alone will deter you from buying the item.

Credit Cards. I keep reading that the average amount of credit card debt ranges from $2,200 to $10,000 per person, not per household, per person. Our society encourages us to spend and to buy. Our society encourages us to have everything NOW.

However, living on purpose is about NOT having debt hang over our heads. How can we focus if we are overwhelmed by debt? The next step to living on purpose is to start paying off your debt. Start by paying whatever you can afford towards your credit card debt, even if it is only an extra $10 of principal per month. Make a list of all the credit cards you have with a balance. List the lowest balance first. Start paying extra on that one until it is paid off. Then, whatever you were paying on that credit card, apply that same amount to the next credit card balance until that is paid in full, and so on.

If you get a raise, take the extra portion and apply to debt and treat the raise as if you never received the money.

Once you begin to pay down debt and you see the results, you will be encouraged to keep striving for the debt free life style.

Living on purpose is about living within your means — spending less than what you are bringing home.

If you have not attended a Dave Ramsey "Financial Peace" course, then I recommend you do. If you are married, attend the course with your spouse. You can go to www.daveramsey.com and find a class offered close to your home.

My husband and I have "business meetings" where we will go over how we spent our money last month and how we want to spend it the following month. Since I am the money manager in our home, I tell him, "it is time for our business meeting and there will be no weeping, wailing and gnashing of teeth." He laughs. This is my way of saying, we will do this in a civilized manner with no raising of voices and no one getting upset.

## 6. Take Care Physically

One of the things I value is my health. Since I have recently been diagnosed with osteoporosis of the spine, working out with weights is even more important to me. My goal is to workout four times a week; that includes 30 minutes of weights and 25 minutes of walking on the treadmill, each time.

I also try to eat right. I eat healthy and drink lots of water. When my husband was diagnosed five years ago with diabetes, he wanted me to attend a nutrition class. The one thing that really stuck in my mind from that class is: portions. We, as Americans, eat too much food in one sitting.

For example, a portion of a piece of meat is the size of a deck of cards. A portion of a starch is ½ cup. A portion of vegetable is ½ cup. When my husband and I go out to eat now, we normally split a plate to keep from eating too much. It is also much cheaper that way, especially when we both drink water.

You cannot live on purpose if you are not taking care of yourself. Taking care of yourself physically means exercising, eating right, drinking plenty of water, and getting enough sleep. All of these are important to living on purpose and feeling well. If you do not take care of yourself, you cannot take care of others.

One of the books I recommend to my coaching clients is "Rev it Up" by Tammy Beasley. This can be purchased on Amazon or on www.revitupfitness.com. "Rev it Up" compares our body to a car engine. It is the best book I have read that explains how our body works and what it actually needs to function. It also has step by step actions to keep on track.

7. **Find a Mentor**

"He who walks with the wise, becomes WISE!"—
words from King Solomon, the wealthiest king in the world EVER
Proverbs 13:20

If you were to choose someone that you admire, who would that be? Name three people that you admire:

_____

_____

_____

What is it about that person that appeals to you?

Treat that person you admire to lunch and pick their brain. Ask that person if she or he would be your mentor. I am sure they would be honored that you asked.

Continue to ask people you meet questions. Surround yourself with smart people, and more specifically, people who are smarter than you. Surround yourself with people who share your same values.

Mentors can and will hold you accountable to what you are working toward. Mentors are good examples to follow.

## 8.   Design a Vision Poster
Making a vision poster has got to be my favorite of all the 10 steps and the most fun!

It was February 1998 when four of us girls went to Seaside, Florida for a girls' weekend. Seaside is called the new urbanism way of life. It is a small town with a grocery store, post office, and businesses — a place where you can live, work, and play. It is a cute town located between Destin and Panama City on the Florida Panhandle. It is known for its pastel color houses with tin roofs and white picket fences. Cars are discouraged from driving on the cobblestone streets.  People usually get around town by walking or riding a bicycle.

Remember I told you earlier that while looking through magazines, a beach house really spoke to me and I wanted to own one? Well, here's how it started. Late one evening, the four of us were walking the streets of Seaside and I just blurted out, "I want a beach house." My friend, Morri, said, "I do too." Then we started thinking about how to make this happen.   The rest of the weekend, Morri and I drove around the area to look for properties. I narrowed it down to three neighborhoods and wanted to come back to the beach with my husband to research a little bit further and to get his input.

When I came home from our girls' weekend, I bought a big piece of poster board at the local grocery store and sat down in the middle of our living room with magazines, scissors, and glue.

I had paper, magazines, etc. sprawled out around me when my husband walks through and says, "What are you doing?"

"I am making a vision poster," I said.

"A vision poster, what is your vision?" he asked.

"I want a place at the beach." (there, I said it again)

My husband's response was "Yeah, right." I could tell by his tone that he thought I was insane. At this point in my husband's life, he was not much of a beach person. How in the world was I going to make THIS happen?

I finished my poster, took it to work and hung it up where I could look at it all of the time! Here is a photo of my vision poster:

After making the poster, Tim and I planned our next trip to the beach. We toured the three neighborhoods that I liked and narrowed it down to one. That weekend, we walked that neighborhood and found a lot for sale. As we were walking, we met a builder who was working on one of the homes in the neighborhood. We told him we were interested in buying a lot. He owned one of the homes in the neighborhood. The more we talked to him, the more we got excited about building a home. We made an offer on the lot that weekend before we left.

After we came home, the builder kept calling us. He found out that we made an offer on the lot and wanted to talk to us about building on that lot which was located right next door to his house. Tim, my husband, who is a mechanical engineer (not an architect), decided he wanted to design the home. That was OK with me because I wanted him to be a big part of this dream and to want it as much as I did. We went back to the beach and met with the builder. The builder took Tim's plans and had a draftsman draw the actual blue prints. When the plans arrived in our mailbox, I knew it would not be long before my dream would became a reality.

Tim kept saying, "we will build the beach house in five years." And I would reply, "Yes, dear." However, the builder we had met kept calling and finally convinced Tim that the price of materials would not go down during that 5-year period, that this was a good time to build, and he could start in November.

Finally, Tim agreed and we started the building process. Tim and I moved into our beach house in March of 1999 (13 months after I made the vision poster). Here is a photo of the beach house we built and which Tim designed. It is located in Seagrove which is within walking distance of Seaside, FL.

In the book, "Think and Grow Rich," by Napoleon Hill, he writes this:

"When Edwin C. Barnes, climbed down from the freight train in Orange, NJ, he may have resembled a tramp, but his *thoughts* were those of a *king*!

As he made his way from the railroad tracks to Thomas A. Edison's office, his mind was at work. _He saw himself standing in Edison's presence._ He heard himself asking Mr. Edison for an opportunity to carry out the one consuming obsession of his life, a burning desire to become the business associate of the great inventor.

Barnes' desire was not a *hope*! It was not a *wish*! It was a keen, pulsating desire, which transcended everything else. It was definite.

A few years later, Edwin C. Barnes again stood before Edison, in the same office where he first met the inventor. This time, his desire had been translated into reality. *He was in business with Edison.* The dominating dream of his life had become a reality.

Barnes succeeded because he chose a definite goal, placed all his energy, all his will power, all his effort, everything to back up that goal.

Five years passed before the chance he had been seeking made its appearance. To everyone, except himself, he appeared only another cog in the Edison business wheel, but in his own mind, he was the partner of Edison every minute of the time, from the very day that he first went to work there.

It is a remarkable illustration of the power of a definite desire and visualization. Barnes who won his goal, because he wanted to be a business associate of Mr. Edison more than he wanted anything else. He created a plan by which to attain that purpose."

Mr. Edwin Barnes had a dream. I had a dream. In these two examples, our dreams became a reality. What is your dream? Write it down in the space below. Start with a vision poster. I give you permission to dream. Then form a plan to make it happen.

_____

_____

_____

_____

_____

## 9. Earn to Learn / Learn to Earn

Recently, we needed some administrative help in our office. We had an idea to hire an intern from the local university, someone that we would "pay" in the form of learning and gaining experience. We found a young man named David. David decided that he would come work for us because he was majoring in government cost accounting. He needed experience so that when he graduated, he could include it on his resume and obtain a professional reference. David was a great fit for our organization. He worked part time, less than 20 hours a week for more than one year. He was dedicated.

Soon, David graduated and began interviewing in town with government contractors. David got a job really quickly and beat other college graduates that did not have experience in the field as David. If you ask David today if it was worth it for him to work without being paid so that he could gain the experience, he would say, "absolutely." David was earning to learn.

Perhaps you have a passion to do something new. To give you an example; perhaps you have a passion to work at a florist shop making floral arrangements and being around plants, but you don't think anyone will hire you. Volunteer your time at a nursery or floral shop so that you can learn the profession.

I just finished reading a book called "I Can't Believe I Get Paid to do This!" by Stacey Mayo. In the book, Mayo interviews Lorall Langemeier. Langemeier talks about how she wanted to learn from the best. So she would volunteer her time to work with the best of the best just so she could learn. At the beginning of her career, Loral had a desire to work in the health and wellness profession, and at the time, Dr. Ken Cooper, MPH, MD, was well known for that. He was the founder of the Cooper Aerobics Center in Texas. She volunteered at the Cooper Clinic just to be with the best of the best and to learn.

After creating her own financial freedom and reaching a net worth of $1 million, it was then that Langemeier decided she would start a coaching and seminar company to provide a catalyst for others to reach this same level of success. The company started small with one office in Novato, California in 2002 and within five years grew to a $19 million dollar company. During that time, the organization expanded to its current size which includes three locations: Novato, California; South Lake Tahoe, Nevada; and Carson City, Nevada. For more information on Langemeier, go to her website: www.loral-langemeier.com.

## 10. Hire a Life Coach

Life coaching is a fairly new profession. Coaching works because the client and coach become a team focusing on the client's goals and what the client needs to do to obtain those goals. Together, as a team, they accomplish more than the client would alone.

With a coach, the client takes more action, thinks bigger, and gets the job done, because of the accountability the coach provides. The coach becomes the cheerleader. Coaching can be used with a personal situation or a professional situation.

I work with women between the ages of 40 – 60. A woman who says, "I know there is something more out there for me."

The benefits they receive while working with me include:

o   Learn how to ask for what you want and get it
o   Learn how to get out of bed in the morning feeling good about yourself
o   Renew your spirit with more energy and more peace
o   Recognize the value and confidence that you already possess
o   Learn how to rely on God to open your path and to reveal your authenticity
o   Find direction, purpose, and pursue your passion

People often ask me what is the difference between coaching and counseling? Coaching is moving the client forward while counseling focuses on dealing with the past. You should interview your coach before signing up. A lot of coaches will give you a free 30 minute session to give you the "feel" of what it is all about. Make sure you and your coach are a good fit. Some questions to ask your coach would include:

- How long have you been a coach?
- Do you have any testimonials I can view?
- What is your expertise in coaching?
- What outcomes can I expect?
- Will we work over the phone or in person?
- How many sessions do I get with you?

Go to my website www.coachmiriam.com to learn more about coaching. You can also Google the International Coaching Federation (ICF) to find out more about coaching.

## In Summary

The 10 steps to Living on Purpose include:

1. Take Inventory of your strengths and your weaknesses
2. Be still. Be quiet
3. Invest in Yourself
4. Set Priorities
5. Control Cash Flow
6. Take Care Physically
7. Find A Mentor
8. Design a Vision Poster
9. Earn to Learn / Learn to Earn
10. Hire A Coach

Of these 10 mentioned, which one is the most doable for you? Write it down.

_____

When will you begin to work on this item?  I will begin on _____(date)

I will work on this task every day, every week, once a month.  (circle one)

I will find an accountability partner if need be to keep me on track.

My plan will consist of:

_____

_____

_____

# The Real Deal

I cannot write this book without telling you about the "Real Deal." To tell you the truth, the real deal to living life on purpose for me is to have Jesus Christ in the center of my life — to include my Heavenly Father in all that I do.

I was raised in a family that valued going to church and having a personal relationship with Jesus Christ. As a child I grew up watching my parents serve and contribute in numerous ways to the community or to the church. This made a huge impression on me. My fondest memory was going out one night with my dad when I was about 7 years old. We had a box of food to deliver to one of his employees who was struggling financially. It was Christmas time and they did not have enough money to provide a nice dinner for their family. Instead of ringing the doorbell and waiting for them to answer and hand them the box, my dad decided we would hide behind the bush and watch. My dad placed me behind a bush, I was literally lying on the ground and watching from a distance. He placed the box of food on the front step, rang the doorbell and ran to where I was behind the bush. We waited and watched. I remember to this day how my heart rate sped up and pounded in my chest with excitement as I waited. They opened their door and found the food with no idea who had brought it. As far as I know, it is still a secret today.

My parents fed the homeless. My parents opened up their home to teenagers to give them a safe haven and to play games. On Sunday after church my mom would feed soldiers from the local army base, who attended our worship service, and then after lunch our front yard became a football field. The list goes on. To this day my siblings and I are all involved in our individual local church, teaching bible lessons or serving in some capacity.

Our family attended a southern Baptist church located in Eatontown, New Jersey. I always got a kick out of that, living in the North and attending a southern Baptist church. The church was small, as you can image, only around 200 members. This is where I heard bible stories and heard sermons on how God had a plan for my life.

It was my mom who taught me about faith. At a very young age, I would come home from school and she would tell me how God worked in her life that day. I remember one incident in particular. Since we did not have a lot of money, mom would make our clothes. Her sewing machine was old and it broke. Knowing that she could not get replacement parts or could not pay to have it repaired, she prayed over her sewing machine. She asked God to help her fix her sewing machine.

After taking a break, she resumed sewing and the sewing machine worked! She was able to finish. She was so excited about that, she couldn't help but tell me how God had repaired her sewing machine. Did God repair it? I have no idea. But here is what made such an impression on me — that mom relied on God to help her with everyday tasks, and because of her faith, all things worked for the good for those that love the Lord. We also saw her pray over the washing machine, the car, and our pets. Nothing was too mundane to bring to the Lord and ask for help.

Recently, I was sitting at my mother's dining room table working away at a water color painting, having the best time. Mother asks, "How did you know to follow your passion?" I told her that it started with journaling. It is about listening to what God is revealing to you – teaching you – experimenting with new ideas.

I don't know where you are in this "God" thing. Maybe you have been hurt by a "Christian" or by the "church." Or maybe you believe that being a

"Christian" is all about rules, when actually it is freedom. I can only tell you what I have experienced and what I know.

Jesus came that we might have life and have it with *abundance*. There is a story that Jesus tells in the book of John, chapter 10 about the sheep and the shepherd. The sheep recognized the shepherd's voice. The shepherd enters through the gate to take the sheep in and out. However, the thief comes in the night, over the wall to kill, destroy, and steal the sheep.

Living life on purpose means making the choice to follow the shepherd and listening to His voice. If we don't choose the shepherd, then by DEFAULT we choose the thief. In this parable, the shepherd is Jesus Christ and the thief is Satan. There are only two choices. Although a relationship with Jesus may seem like rules about obeying the word (Bible), following a Christian life will bring peace, confidence, and freedom. Following Satan will bring you to misery, sadness, and permanent death.

You might say, "Well, you don't know the life that I have been given; you don't know the pain that I have had." And you are correct. I do not know your struggles, pain, or horrible experiences. But God Almighty does. He is the master healer. He is the one that has created you for a purpose. He needs you in this world of anger, sin, and pain. He needs you with all your bumps, bruises, and experiences. It is all of those experiences that have shaped you into who you are today. He needs you to bring back into the world your abilities, your skill set, your joy, and your goodness. One of the names God is given in the scriptures is "Redeemer." He can even take the worst experiences and turn them around for the good. God needs you to get "unstuck" from your story. The story you have in your head that says I am not good enough. That story you have in your head that says I am not worthy. Your Heavenly Father, God Almighty wants you to rewrite your story. The story that says, "You are worthy, daughter. I have come that you might have life and have it with abundance. For I am with you always." Rewrite your story the way God would write your story, not Satan.

The experiences that you have gone through are there to help you with others who are walking the same journey — to share and mentor others to have the life of living on purpose.

If we are doing what we have been designed to do, whatever that is, it comes easy. It is natural. For instance, solving an engineering problem may come easy to someone who loves this type of work. They just love figuring out the problem. Time flies because it is so easy. To someone else, trying to figure out that same engineering problem requires patience and time. It probably drains them to figure out this problem. It does not come naturally and they fuss and fume as they work on this project. Time drags on and they can't wait until quitting time. Does that make sense?

In the book, "The Cure for the Common Life," author Max Lucado says that 70% of working adults haven't found their skill set and don't find meaning in their work.

This is what I know. When you start "living on purpose" and you have a plan, life is rewarding. Life *does* have meaning and purpose. If you are settling and just taking what falls into your lap, then you become more susceptible to becoming sick, gaining weight, and getting very frustrated.

I believe that when you start living on purpose and are working in your skill set, you look forward to the day. When you live on purpose with Christ at the center and have a relationship with Him, doors will open up that don't normally open. People step into your life that you need to meet. You hear words on the radio or you hear words from a friend that you needed to hear at just the right time, just the right place. God finds "favor" in you.

During my journey, I have had some incredible experiences. People have stepped into my life that I needed to meet. People have encouraged me with words that I needed to hear at just the right time. I have met some incredible women. Some of these women have encouraged me to pursue my passion including writing this book. With my Life by Design business, I sometimes get discouraged and want to close the business, which happens to many entrepreneurs. When I am feeling this way, I talk to God about it, and then, all of a sudden, out of the blue, I will get a phone call from a woman I met several months ago at a particular event and she will want me to coach her through Life by Design. Then the joy of this business and the desire comes back to me and re-energizes me to keep moving forward with the business.

I have found my gifts of training, speaking, and encouraging. I have the opportunity to do this with my job and volunteer work. This brings me great joy to help others be the best they can be. I even have the privilege and opportunity to tutor at the local learning center.

## Special note from author:

If you haven't surrendered your life to Christ and are ready to follow him, follow these steps:

1. Acknowledge that you have sinned and fallen short of the glory of God. (Romans 3:23)
2. Ask for forgiveness for your sins and for forgiveness for your disobedience to God.
3. Acknowledge that Jesus Christ is the Son of God. (John 3:16)
4. Be baptized (full immersion) for the forgiveness of your sins (Acts 2:38). This is an outward expression of what has happened inside.
5. Tell someone about your experience; be a witness.

After that, find a church that teaches truth from the Bible. Visit various churches and find one that fits your personality, a place where you can learn and grow.

Here is a simple prayer of faith that you can use as a guide:

Dear Heavenly Father – Creator of all things. I know I am not walking with you right now. I know I have been disobedient to your will. I have hurt you and others. I hate living my life without you. I have made a mess of things.

I acknowledge you as my Lord and Savior. I know that Jesus Christ is your son and has died on the cross for my mistakes, my sins. Please forgive me for my sins. I ask that you come into my heart and fill me with your joy. All of these things, I pray in your precious and holy name. *Amen.*

You can offer this prayer in silence by yourself. Or you can pray this prayer with a friend. The choice is up to you. Your Heavenly Father is waiting and will listen.

Last, but not least, be baptized. Why baptism? Because it is the symbol of obedience to God. Baptism washes away all of the ugly and creates a new person when you come up out of the water – a new person with a new way of thinking, behaving, and talking. If you want a fresh start, be baptized. If you want to become a new creation, be baptized. Find a church home for continued fellowship and support. You will desperately need to be with people who believe in you and share the same values.

# Breathe

We are all walking wounded. We all have a past. We have all made mistakes.

Our past, our mistakes, and our wounds that need healing should not keep us from living a life with abundance *or* living a life with purpose.

It begins with a choice.

Start surrounding yourself with people who are full of life, full of positive energy — people who enjoy living. If you have "naysayers" in your life, or negative people, stay clear of them. If they live in your home, ask them to *stop* with the negative talk. Set your boundaries and decide that life is too short to listen to this and you will not.

Continue to grow. Continue to learn. Don't get stuck in the same ole pattern. Seek out your authentic self. Journal. Spend time alone. Being alone is where you face your true self, because it is here that you are most honest.

Simplify your life. Get rid of the clutter. Buy the "Simple Abundance Book – A Daybook of Comfort and Joy."

Dream. Dream BIG. Make a plan that includes baby steps to move you toward your dream.

This book is full of wonderful ideas on how to live on purpose. I want to encourage you to take advantage of some of these ideas and tips. It will only lead to joy and contentment.  Find an accountability partner and work together.

For me, I am still on this journey of life, journaling, reading, improving, and having a blast!

To me, living on purpose is finding your uniqueness, using that in the workplace, and getting paid for it. Or, perhaps using your uniqueness in a volunteer situation or using your uniqueness as a full-time mom.

Wouldn't it be great if as a result of people living on purpose, there was less drug and alcohol abuse?

Wouldn't it be great if as a result of people living on purpose, there was less anger and domestic abuse?

Wouldn't it be great if as a result of people living on purpose, there was less dependency on drugs?

I have had so much fun sharing my thoughts, my stories, and my journey in this book.  This journey of living on purpose is available to everyone.

Words from Sarah Ban Breathnach tell us that living your authentic life is the most personal form of worship.

Remember words from our Creator,  "For I have come that you may have life and have it with abundance!"  This is a promise from John 10:10.  Amen!

I hope this book has changed your life. I hope this book has set you on a mission to journal, to search, to not live life by default.

Thank you for your time and interest in reading this book.  May the Lord richly bless your life.

Living on Purpose,

Miriam Ezell

www.coachmiriam.com

**<u>Recommended Books that I have read during my journey include:</u>**

**"Cure for The Common Life"** by Max Lucado

**"Dress Your Best"** by Stacy London and Clinton Kelly

**"The Artist's Way"** by Julia Cameron

**"Simple Abundance"** by Sarah Ban Breathnach

**"Do What You Love and The Money will Follow"** by Marsha Sinetar

**"The 10 Laws of Career Reinvention"** by Pamela Mitchell

**"When a Woman Discovers her Dream"** by Cindi McMenamin

**"The Path"** by Laurie Beth Jones

**"Rev it Up Fitness"** by Tammy Beasley

**"I Can't Believe I Get Paid to Do This"** by Stacey Mayo

Where is My Money Going ????

| Date | Description | Income | Home | Groceries | Eating Out | Auto/Gas | Clothes | Recreation | Contributions |
|------|-------------|--------|------|-----------|-----------|----------|---------|------------|---------------|
| 7/1/11 | House Mortgage | | 2,225.00 | | | | | | |
| 7/1/11 | Paycheck | 2,538.15 | | | | | | | |
| 7/1/11 | Church contribution | | | | | | | | 255.00 |
| 7/2/11 | Grocery Store | | | 158.99 | | | | | |
| 7/2/11 | Mexican Restaurant | | | | 25.43 | | | | |
| 7/3/11 | Ruby Tuesdays | | | | 10.15 | | | | |
| 7/4/11 | Subway | | | | 11.03 | | | | |
| 7/5/11 | Grocery Store | | | 176.02 | | | | | |
| 7/6/11 | Gas Station | | | | | 52.00 | | | |
| 7/7/11 | Gas Station | | | | | 36.00 | | | |
| 7/7/11 | Movie Theatre | | | | | | | 35.00 | |
| 7/7/11 | DSW Shoes | | | | | | 53.44 | | |
| 7/8/11 | Paycheck - wife | 1,005.18 | | | | | | | |
| 7/8/11 | Church contribution | | | | | | | | 100.00 |
| 7/9/11 | Starbuck's | | | | 4.39 | | | | |
| 7/10/11 | Car Payment | | | | | 322.00 | | | |
| 7/10/11 | Car Payment | | | | | 257.00 | | | |
| 7/10/11 | Ruby Tuesdays | | | | 32.35 | | | | |
| 7/12/11 | Gas Station | | | | | 56.00 | | | |
| 7/13/11 | Starbuck's | | | | 4.39 | | | | |
| 7/13/11 | Gas Station | | | | | 32.00 | | | |
| 7/15/11 | Church contribution | | | | | | | | 255.00 |
| 7/15/11 | Paycheck | 2,538.15 | | | | | | | |
| 7/15/11 | AMEX c/c | | | 155.00 | 125.00 | 245.00 | | | |
| 7/15/11 | Discover | | | | | | 350.00 | | |
| 7/16/11 | Grocery Store | | | 206.99 | | | | | |
| 7/16/11 | O'Charley's | | | | 15.32 | | | | |
| 7/16/11 | Chevron | | | | | 55.00 | | | |
| 7/17/11 | Home Depot | | 254.45 | | | | | | |
| 7/17/11 | Chevron | | | | | 35.00 | | | |
| 7/18/11 | Starbuck's | | | | 4.39 | | | | |
| 7/22/11 | Paycheck - wife | 1,005.18 | | | | | | | |
| 7/23/11 | Church contribution | | | | | | | | 105.00 |
| 7/23/11 | Utilities | | 178.95 | | | | | | |
| 7/23/11 | Water | | 33.56 | | | | | | |
| 7/25/11 | AT&T | | 89.10 | | | | | | |
| 7/25/11 | Chevron | | | | | 47.00 | | | |
| 7/25/11 | Cable Company | | 115.10 | | | | | | |
| 7/26/11 | Publix | | | 227.22 | | | | | |
| 7/26/11 | Texaco | | | | | 33.00 | | | |
| 7/26/11 | Ruby Tuesdays | | | | 56.40 | | | | |
| 7/27/11 | PF Changs | | | | 37.58 | | | | |
| 7/27/11 | Books a Million | | | | | | | 56.22 | |
| 7/28/11 | Belk's | | | | | | 335.67 | | |
| | total Income | 7,086.66 | 2,896.16 | 924.22 | 326.43 | 1,170.00 | 739.11 | 91.22 | 715.00 |
| | total expenses | (6,862.14) | | | | | | | |
| | income - expenses | 224.52 | | | | | | | |

# ABOUT MIRIAM

Miriam Ezell is a small business owner and creator of the "Live on Purpose Empowerment Series for Women." In addition to being a life coach, she is a motivational speaker.

Life by Design was created to transform women's lives who desire to change. Her clients include women between the ages of 40 – 60. A woman who says, "I know there is something more out there for me," a woman seeking more time, more energy, more peace, and more purpose.

Miriam lives in Madison, Alabama with her husband, Tim, a NASA engineer. Miriam also enjoys time at the beach and being creative with water color, mixed media and quilting.

Made in the USA
Charleston, SC
18 January 2013